PERVERSE INCENTIVES

PERVERSE INCENTIVES

The Neglect of Social Technology in the Public Sector

Theodore Caplow

PRAEGER

Westport, Connecticut
London

Library of Congress Cataloging-in-Publication Data

Caplow, Theodore.
    Perverse incentives : the neglect of social technology in the
public sector / Theodore Caplow.
       p. cm.
    Includes bibliographical references and index.
    ISBN 0–275–94911–7 (alk. paper).—ISBN 0–275–94933–8 (pbk.)
    1. Social service—United States. 2. Human services—United
States. 3. Criminal justice, Administration of—United States.
    I. Title.
    HV91.C35 1994
    361.973—dc20   94–2981

British Library Cataloguing in Publication Data is available.

Library of Congress Catalog Card Number: 94–2981
ISBN: 0–275–94911–7
      0–275–94933–8 (pbk.)

First published in 1994

Praeger Publishers, 88 Post Road West, Westport, CT 06881
An imprint of Greenwood Publishing Group, Inc.

Printed in the United States of America

The paper used in this book complies with the
Permanent Paper Standard issued by the National
Information Standards Organization (Z39.48–1984).

10 9 8 7 6 5 4 3 2 1

CONTENTS

PERVERSE INCENTIVES

I

CARELESS DESIGN

INTRODUCTION

The deterioration of the American welfare state since 1970 has been one of the major events of our history. This has not yet been fully recognized. All of us know that there are serious problems in the health care, education, welfare, criminal justice and liability systems, but most of us do not understand why they developed and how they are interconnected.

These problems are peculiar to the United States. No other advanced industrial nation is now so clumsy and inefficient in caring for the health of its people, educating children, alleviating poverty, controlling crime or compensating accident victims.[1]

Until recently we Americans did most of these things well and the rest of the world struggled to catch up with us. Now we do them badly. At least five of the big social programs on which we depend to establish justice, insure domestic tranquility and promote the general welfare have largely broken down.

Consider some numbers:

— From $2 billion in 1970, the cost of Medicaid went to about $115 billion in 1992.[2] By then, the program provided coverage to fewer than half of the poor, and not very good coverage either.

— In cross-national studies of educational achievement, American students rank consistently toward the bottom.[3]
— More than two-thirds of all black births are now to unmarried mothers.[4] Nearly all of these unmarried mothers are poor, and nearly all of their children will be raised in poverty.
— In the ten years between 1980 and 1990, the number of sentenced prisoners per 100,000 U.S. residents rose from 160 to 282.[5] About half as many more were in jail. These rates are about ten times as high as the incarceration rates for Germany or France and are still rising by about 20 percent a year.
— Between 1970 and 1990, the malpractice premiums paid by some American physicians increased by 20,000 percent. But fewer than 1 percent of the patients injured by medical treatment received any compensation.[6]

CARELESS DESIGN

These unfavorable trends are the direct results of government programs that aggravate the ills they are supposed to cure. The programs were carelessly designed, and in each case the great defect was that the designers, full of good intentions, violated the elementary principles of social technology.

There were too many designers, and they worked at cross-purposes: Congress and congressional staff members, the White House, federal regulators, the legislatures of 50 states, the federal courts, the state courts, and state and local agencies, as well as the interest groups that influenced them all.

Most of the designers were legislators, judges, regulators and lobbyists with short-term perspectives. They did not understand the elementary principles of social technology and did not recognize their own ignorance. They were like primitive tribesmen trying to repair an airplane without knowing anything about metallurgy or the principles of flight.

Most of them did not have accurate pictures of the behavior they were trying to change or the context in which that behavior occurred. Consequently, they had no clear idea of how a given change in the rules of the game might influence the actions of the players.

When they infused new federal or state money into an existing system, they seldom stopped to consider how it might affect the existing price structure, or the relative power of professionals and clients, or whether it might offer irresistible opportunities for cheating and stealing. When they drafted new rules, they did not consider how the new rules would interact with older rules, or how much they would cost to enforce, or whether they were enforceable at all, or how they could be used for private advantage. They seldom took account of the inevitable differences between a program on paper and the same program in practice. Above all, they never really tried to see the system from the standpoint of the people in the system—welfare mothers, high school teachers, drug dealers, physicians, lawyers. Flying blind as they did, they inadvertently created perverse incentives. The welfare mothers were given good reasons to bear more children, the high school teachers to give up on homework, the drug dealers to recruit new customers, the physicians to double their fees, the lawyers to sue and sue.

That was not all.

It was, and is, the custom of this country to evaluate social programs by the goodness of their intentions not the goodness of their results. Because there is so little concern with results, it is not customary for legislators and reformers to set specific goals.

It is also the custom of this country to regard American experience as so unique that we cannot profit from the experience of other nations. Although other advanced industrial nations have been providing the same social services for a long time, we have neither copied their successes nor avoided their mistakes. Indeed, we have not even been willing to learn from our own experience. The large body of knowledge accumulated by social research about motivation, learning, behavior control, family structure, bureaucratic processes and many other relevant matters is seldom consulted by the careless designers.

Since they habitually ignore the probability that the changes they introduce will have unintended consequences, they are very slow to react when those consequences occur. As often as not, nobody seems to notice when the unexpected costs of new programs wipe out the intended benefits. Not one of our major national programs provides adequate feedback.

Because of inadequate feedback, and because of the built-in indifference to results, the careless designers do not respond appropriately to breakdowns. Most of the current problems of the health care, education, welfare, justice and liability systems were evident years ago but neglect has made them much harder to deal with than they would have been when they first appeared.

These habits still persist, of course, and it is possible to identify newer programs, such as the federal child care program, created by the federal Child Care and Development Block Grant of 1990, that are destined to fail for similar reasons. It is loaded with perverse incentives that are likely to raise the cost and lower the quality of child care in the United States.[7]

A THUMBNAIL HISTORY

Each of our failing human service systems is a vast network of public, semiprivate and private organizations staffed by professionals and licensed by government. Some of these organizations have long histories, going back to colonial times, but all of them have been thoroughly redesigned since 1960.

A full description of these systems is beyond the scope of this book and probably beyond the reach of the human mind. They are huge and widely dispersed. Their structures are intricate, their records are scattered and their procedures are often inexplicable.

The rules of the game in these systems are made and enforced by all three branches of government—executive, legislative and judicial—and at all three levels of government—national, state and local. In all five systems, the costs to the public have recently soared out of sight, without any reduction of the costs borne by private citizens.

Many Americans are so accustomed to the hardships imposed on them as they seek health care or education or personal safety that they accept such abuses as normal. But I will try to show that these systems malfunction only because they are badly designed.

Many of their problems can be traced to the quiet revolution in the American form of government that took place between 1960 and the present. In 1960, huge areas of collective action—health care, education, criminal justice, civil litigation, infant care, occupational safety, personnel procedures, the regulation of sexual relationships, child care, environmental protection, music and art, historic preservation, the content of advertising and the design of consumer products—were still outside of the federal orbit. By now, they have all been brought inside.[8]

Because this revolution was implemented piecemeal, by super-imposing a new layer of federal control over the state, local and institutional authorities that were already in place, no economies of scale were achieved. The governments of the 50 states responded to the encroachment of the federal government not by reducing their own activities but by encroaching in turn on local governments and private institutions, which, instead of contracting, expanded under pressure. Every public and private institution became answerable to regulatory agencies on all three levels: local, state and federal.

Under the new regime of overlapping jurisdictions, enormous amounts of public money were poured into government programs that were designed in haste, installed without reflection and operated without attention to results.

The result was a massive escalation of costs without corresponding benefits. Between 1960 and 1994, health care costs outraced inflation by 5 to 1, education costs by 3 to 1, welfare costs by 2 to 1, criminal justice costs by 3 to 1 and liability costs by 6 to 1.[9]

The public got very little for its money.

FIVE FAILING SYSTEMS

In the health care system, there were more diagnostic procedures, more prescriptions and more operations, but the general health of the population did not improve, and by now the United States has lower life expectancy, higher infant mortality and more infectious disease than the other rich countries. The injuries incurred by patients in the course of medical treatment, the volume of unnecessary surgery and the incidence of prescription-induced drug addiction all rose to record levels. The average physician has a higher net income than a Justice of the U.S. Supreme Court and the pharmaceutical industry has wider profit margins than any other, while the costs of routine health care have risen beyond what the nation can afford. Medicare and Medicaid are the most costly social programs in the entire world, but more than half of U.S. families in poverty were not covered by Medicaid in 1994 and the elderly paid a larger proportion of their own incomes for health care than they did before Medicare existed. Before reform, the health care system took about 14 percent of the gross national

product—more than twice the average of other industrial countries; after reform, it will take even more.

The U.S. educational system has three major problems: (1) a
trend of cost escalation that continues unabated, (2) the inability of
the public schools to educate their students as well as foreign
schools educate theirs and (3) the loss of order and civility in many
schools.

The U.S. welfare system centers on the payment of living allowances to unmarried low-income mothers. It is unintentionally but
efficiently designed to break up existing families, prevent the
formation of new ones, encourage extramarital childbearing, penalize the working poor, discourage saving and home ownership,
and perpetuate itself. It is largely responsible for single-parent
households, unsafe neighborhoods and disorderly schools, and for
their concentration in large metropolitan areas. There is nothing at
all that this system does well.

As to the criminal justice system, the United States now has
more prisoners per capita than any other country in the world. The
prisons are lawless and dangerous places that do not even pretend
to rehabilitate their inmates. The system is racially selective. It
targets young black and Hispanic men, with devastating consequences for their families. The adjudication of cases is slow, clumsy
and inconsistent. There is little proportionality between crimes and
punishments. And the costs are out of control.

The liability system that compensates individuals for personal
injury has been redesigned in the past two decades to eliminate
most of the guidelines that formerly determined whether the malice or negligence of one citizen had caused damage to another. The
system now operates on the principle that if someone suffers an
injury, affluent others should be made to pay compensation even
if their connection with the injury was remote and their actions
innocent. There are no rules at all about what constitutes fair
compensation. The procedures for obtaining compensation are
slow, extremely expensive and generally unpredictable. The great
majority of victims are not compensated at all. Most of the money
paid into the system never gets to victims. The risk of being sued
inhibits all sorts of useful activities. The ever-rising insurance
burden increases the cost of virtually everything produced in the
United States.

These defective systems are interconnected in many ways and their defects are mutually reinforcing. The failures of the welfare system undermine the public schools. The failures of the schools feed the mills of criminal justice. The aberrations of the liability system stimulate medical inflation.

PERVERSE INCENTIVES

Perverse incentives are rewards and punishments that are built into a system and block the achievement of that system's goals. Built into Medicare, for example, are powerful incentives for health care providers to raise their fees continually, thus frustrating the goal of providing affordable medical care for the elderly. Built into the welfare system are punishments for unmarried mothers who marry or take jobs, thus assuring that they and their children will not escape from poverty. Built into the criminal justice system are lavish rewards for drug-dealing that guarantee a steady stream of recruits for the criminal underworld. Built into the educational system are ingenious punishments for teachers and students who take learning too seriously. Built into the liability system are incentives for insurers continually to reduce the protection the system is supposed to provide.

There have been, in recent years, numerous attempts to reform these systems—cost-containment measures that were supposed to halt the escalation of physicians' fees, job training programs for welfare mothers, the expansion of police resources for the war on drugs, competency testing of teachers and legislative restriction of tort liability. These measures were not even moderately successful. In each case, the principles of social technology continued to be ignored and the perverse incentives that result from that neglect were either left untouched or reinforced.

There is nothing mysterious about the principles of social technology that we will review in the next chapter. They are acknowledged and respected in most human enterprises most of the time because the penalties for ignoring them are so heavy. But Congress and the federal courts march to a different tune.

CAVEATS

It is quite impossible to write a book about problems as urgent as these without sometimes being overtaken by events. As this is written, the outcome of the Clinton administration's effort to reform the health care system is still uncertain, but it is highly probable that some plan of health care reform will be enacted. If that plan eventually succeeds in removing the perverse incentives for providers to raise their prices that are built into the existing health care system, it will be an augury of great hope for the future of this country. But even if the plan is unable to check medical inflation, it will change the terms of the debate. It will not, however, change the history recounted in the chapter on health care or the dynamics of the relationship between perverse incentives and system failure.

There are plans afoot for educational reforms at all levels, including the application of information technology to primary and secondary education and the installation of a national testing system. These plans are rather modest so far but they may become more ambitious during the legislative process. If they do, the chapter on education would need to be revised.

The Clinton administration has also announced its intention to reform welfare by expanded job training and stricter eligibility rules. These futile measures have been tried many times before. They will not affect the perverse incentives for poor women to bear children and remain unmarried that are built into the existing system. Job training is futile because the typical client, when trained and fully employed, would be no better off than before. Stricter eligibility rules create administrative overhead and individual hardships but do not have much effect on the case load. The chapter on welfare should survive unscathed.

In the chapter on criminal justice, I identify drug prohibition as the root cause of that system's problems, particularly the mania for incarceration that carries so many social costs and so few social benefits. The only imaginable solution is to decriminalize drug trafficking but that step is not imminent. The great majority of elected officials, both Democrat and Republican, are drug war hawks; the doves are small voices crying in the wilderness. Events will probably not overtake me here.

Likewise in the liability system, there is as yet no movement for general reform. The medical malpractice branch of that system is the one most likely to be modified, because of its intimate connection with health care costs. The most likely measure is a limitation of patients' rights to recover damages for noneconomic losses. The least likely measure, for the time being, is one that would offer compensation to a larger proportion of injured patients. The other parts of the chapter on liability may not need revision so soon.

The reader should also be warned that this small book does not pretend to tell the whole story of these five large systems. Their social, economic and political ramifications are endless and can be viewed from many different perspectives. The approach taken here is deliberately narrow, focussed on the design defects that prevent these systems from achieving their ostensible goals. This narrow focus excludes more topics than I can count but it illuminates the question that applied sociology aspires to answer, "What should be done?"

NOTES

1. For the past several years, a group of us have been following recent social trends in about a dozen developed countries, as part of an international project. We have found that many of the major trends that transformed American society between 1960 and 1990 were shared with other developed nations, but that the deterioration of the major human service systems was peculiar to this country. The U.S. report of this project was presented in a thick book, Theodore Caplow, Howard M. Bahr, John Modell and Bruce A. Chadwick, *Recent Social Trends in the United States 1960–1990* (Frankfurt am Main: Campus Verlag, Montreal: McGill-Queens University Press, 1991) and discussed in a thin one, Theodore Caplow, *American Social Trends* (San Diego, CA: Harcourt Brace Jovanovich, 1991). Comparable national profiles have been published for Quebec, West Germany, and France as follows: Simon Langlois, Jean-Paul Baillargeon, Gary Caldwell, Guy Frechet, Madeleine Gauthier and Jean-Pierre Simard, *Recent Social Trends in Quebec 1960–1990* (Frankfurt am Main: Campus Verlag, Montreal: McGill-Queens University Press, 1991); Wolfgang Glatzer, Karl-Otto Hondrich, Heinz Herbert Noll, Karin Stiehr and Barbara Worndl, *Recent Social Trends in West Germany 1960–1990* (Frankfurt am Main: Campus Verlag, Montreal: McGill-Queens University Press, 1992); Michel Forsé, Jean-Pierre Jaslin, Yannick Lemel, Henri Mendras, Denis Stoclet and Jean-Hughes Dechaux, *Recent Social*

Trends in France 1960–1990 (Frankfurt am Main: Campus Verlag, Montreal McGill-Queens University Press, 1993). Similar volumes for half a dozen other countries are in preparation.

2. Kaiser Commission on Medicaid, 1991; Associated Press (January 1993).

3. National Commission on Excellence in Education, *A Nation at Risk* (Washington, DC: GPO, 1983).

4. *Statistical Abstract of the United States 1993*, Table 89.

5. U.S. Bureau of Justice Statistics: *Prisons and Prisoners in the United States*, NCJ-137002 (1992); *Correctional Populations in the United States 1988*, NCJ-124280 (1991); *Prisoners 1925–1981* (1991); *National Update*, 1, no. 3 NCJ-133097 (1992).

6. Harvard Medical Practice Study, *Patients, Doctors, Lawyers: Medical Injury, Malpractice Litigation, and Patient Compensation* (Cambridge, MA: President and Fellows of Harvard College, 1990). See also Patricia M. Danzon, *Medical Malpractice: Theory, Evidence and Public Policy* (Cambridge, MA: Harvard University Press, 1985) and "Liability for Medical Malpractice," *Journal of Economic Perspectives* 5, no. 3 (Summer 1991): 51–69.

7. Aside from the usual perverse incentive to providers to raise their prices indefinitely because of the bottomless pocket of the federal government, is the new child care program that creates powerful incentives for the informal providers who presently furnish most of the nation's preschool care at low cost and in a generally satisfactory way to quit the field in favor of for-profit child care centers with numerous quality and safety problems. See, among other sources, National Center for Health Statistics, *Child Care Arrangements 1988*, Advance Data no. 187 (Hyattsville, MD: U.S. Dept. of Health and Human Services, 1990); U.S. Congress Senate, Committee on the Judiciary, *Protecting Children in Day Care: Building a National Background Check System*, Serial No. J-102–44 (Washington, DC: GPO, 1991); National Center for Education Statistics, *Experiences in Child Care and Early Childhood Programs of First and Second Graders*, NCES 92–005 (Washington, DC: National Center for Education Statistics, 1992).

8. This revolution was achieved not by amending the Constitution but by reinterpreting it, sometimes by means of judicial rulings that found new meanings in that venerable document, and sometimes by buying new powers with federal funds. The amendments passed between 1960 and 1990, the 23rd, 24th and 25th, dealt respectively with presidential voting in the District of Columbia, poll taxes and presidential disability, and were unrelated to the transformation discussed here.

9. Health care expenditures established by the author are based on examination of many different sources. My estimates of educational expenditures omits the costs of private schools. My estimate for welfare

includes Aid to Dependent Children, food stamps and Supplementary Social Security, but excludes Medicaid, which was counted under health care. My estimate for criminal justice includes expenditures for police and corrections only; it does not take account of court costs and legal fees. My estimate for liability is based on the aggregate premiums paid for liability insurance of all kinds. It excludes the increase of court costs and uninsured liability expenses.

2

SOCIAL TECHNOLOGY

To apply social technology to the improvement of an existing system, serious reformers must do the following things:

First, identify a condition that ought to be changed and find its root causes.

Second, design a program to modify that condition in a precisely described way.

Third, imitate success, learn from failure.

Fourth, accept incurred costs.

Fifth, specify the interim measures that are intended to lead to the desired end-condition, give them numerical values and set numerical goals for successive stages of the program in real time.

Sixth, predict the intended effect of each interim measure on the incentives of participants, both agents and clients.

Seventh, install procedures for continuous monitoring that can identify deviations from the program as soon as they occur.

Eighth, calculate in as much detail as possible the projected monetary costs at each stage of the program.

Ninth, predict as carefully as possible the potential negative effects at each stage of the program.

Tenth, revise all projections at regular intervals.

Eleventh, make midcourse corrections as often as necessary.

This style of social action differs from the prevailing American style in several important ways: the resolution of a social problem is visualized as an operational sequence, rather than a single act; the expected benefits are quantified and continuously compared with the expected costs; the divergence of actual from intended results is anticipated and provided for; the incentives of participants are kept in continuous view.

The objection can be raised that this style of social action presupposes a single designer or group of designers who devise and carry out a problem-solving program, while in real life such programs emerge from legislative negotiation and compromise, are set in motion by executive agencies with agendas of their own and are then unpredictably modified by the courts.

These objections are well founded but not conclusive. We already know that we live in an imperfect world but we also know that rational problem solving is possible in that world and that it occurs every day. We can surely hope to reach the same level of competence in the provision of social services as other countries or even to return to our own former level.

Social technology is successfully applied every day by people who open barber shops and hardware stores, found schools and churches, organize baseball teams and garden clubs, plan political campaigns and music festivals or do anything else that involves risk, foresight and the cooperation of others. Almost always, they take existing organizations of the same type as models for their own projects. They may introduce one or two small improvements but they are unlikely to attempt any drastic innovations.

The imitation of successful projects is the simplest and most effective kind of social technology. When the same model has been used hundreds or thousands of times, success is not assured but the requirements for success are easy to identify.

These models come equipped with all the necessary parts and pieces of an operational social system: norms, values, attitudes, tables of organization, divisions of labor, status ladders, roles and role models, measures of input and output, performance criteria, legal rights and obligations. Above all, the appropriate incentives are built in, so that when suitable participants have been recruited, the general congruence of their behavior with the goals of the project can almost be taken for granted.

The models that are widely imitated have survived a long-term process of selection that eliminate ineffective or unstable designs.

The development of brand new models of social organization is a formidable task. Most of them can be expected to fail—either because they do not have adequate incentives to attract and hold participants or because the incentives they generate do not serve the goals of the project.

Good intentions and blind luck are not enough. The development of innovative programs of social action calls for close attention to the outcome of similar and parallel experiments in the past, familiarity with the relevant findings of social research, mechanisms for the continuous monitoring of results, and a firm commitment to trial-and-error.

Even this is not enough unless the goals are clearly specified. Let us linger on this last point for a moment. When goals are expressed only in rhetorical terms (a healthy America, quality education for all) there is no way results can be monitored and midcourse corrections made.

An innovative program of social action is an effort by one set of people (reformers, legislators, bureaucrats, judges) to change the behavior of another set of people (physicians, patients, teachers, pupils, social workers, welfare clients, policemen, street criminals, drug dealers, litigants, underwriters). Since few people take kindly to having their behavior changed, the incentives for them to do so must be very strong. But providing strong incentives for other people is a tricky business, especially when the people whose behavior is to be changed have opportunities to tamper with the program for their own advantage.

The reciprocal demands of a social system and its individual members are always excessive. The system wants more obedience and commitment from the individual than he or she is ever willing to give. Programs of social action never work exactly as planned because no such program is entirely congruent with the private interests of the participants.

The evasion of laws and rules appears with monotonous consistency whenever people are commanded to do things for the benefit of others or for the common good that they consider to be against their own interests or unnecessary or unfair.

The clearest examples involve monetary costs. The norms of their respective reference groups predictably support doctors who circumvent cost-containment rules, teachers who resist computerized instruction, welfare clients who conceal earnings, drug dealers who seek out new users, insurers who cancel the policies of sick claimants.

In social service systems that have become exploitative, every attempt at reform must meet the inevitable fierce resistance of those who are commanded to reduce their earnings or give up their privileges for the benefit of others or for the common good. More often than not, their resistance prevails.

We shall return in a later chapter to the political feasibility of overcoming that resistance. But first we need to look more closely at the problem of applying social technology to the improvement of an existing service system. To do that, serious reformers must first identify a condition that ought to be changed and find its root cause or causes. If one starts with the assumption that the cheating by clients is the principal defect of the welfare system, the chance of effecting any real improvement are virtually nil. If one believes that the great recent surge in the prison population was caused by a great increase of violent crime, there is not much room to maneuver towards a solution. In other words, meaningful reform must start with an accurate description of facts.

The next requirement is to design a program to modify unwanted conditions in a precisely detailed way. Most reform proposals describe the problem in much more detail than the solution. The candidate who promises to get tough on crime never tells us that his program is intended to reduce street crime by 25 percent and property crime by 40 percent over a period of three years. He knows better.

To have internal validity, a reform proposal must propose an objective change to be achieved in real time, not immediately and not in the unspecified future, but step by step from where we are to where we want to be. Unless the proposed effort is set in a calendar and described numerically, it should not be taken seriously. But beware of imitation calendars: "By the year 2000," according to the National Education Summit convoked by President Bush in 1989, "every school in America will be free of drugs and violence and will offer a disciplined environment conducive to learning." What a pitiful hope!

Many projects of social improvement are not really more complicated than building a shed, but what would we think of someone who set out to build a shed without first deciding what its dimensions would be? The absence of realistic imagery is what makes projects like the National Education Summit so forlorn. Without a clear idea of what they were trying to do, how could they go about doing it?

That successful projects should be imitated and unsuccessful ones studied is an obvious, practical rule, but it finds no place in the culture of the American welfare state. The Civilian Conservation Corps was perhaps the most successful project of the New Deal. It has not been imitated since. Job training for welfare mothers has been tried repeatedly without any favorable results. It is the centerpiece of a dozen current proposals. For various reasons, the death penalty has become unenforceable in the United States; only a minuscule fraction of those sentenced are ever executed. The extension of the death penalty to new offenses is a major feature of current legislation. States that instituted merit pay for teachers found that it had a deleterious effect on morale. Other states are now installing it. Workers' compensation has effectively compensated the victims of industrial accidents for half a century. Proposals to handle medical injuries in the same way have gotten nowhere.

The least comfortable principle of social technology is that which tells the serious reformer that incurred costs must be accepted, or to put it more broadly, that past errors have irreversible consequences. Without a badly designed welfare system, there would never have been seven million fatherless families in the United States, but no reform of that system would now cause those families to disappear. If all the defects of the welfare system were remedied tomorrow, their consequences would nevertheless persist far into the twenty-first century.

If, let us say, the health care system is successfully reformed, the United States will continue to have higher health care costs than any other advanced industrial country and aggregate results that are not quite as good. Health care now consumes 14 percent of our gross domestic product. In another few years, if left unchecked, that might go above 20 percent. No other country now spends more than 10 percent. But we will not get back to 10 percent. The best that current reformers hope to do is arrest the growth at 17 or 18 percent and live with the very high costs that have been built into the system. They cannot be shrunk back to a reasonable level in the foreseeable future.

The weight of incurred costs is even more dramatically illustrated by drug abuse. If the worst features of drug prohibition were removed it is quite likely that the use of drugs would increase rather than decrease. It is even possible that the decriminalization of drugs might temporarily increase the incidence of violent crime. The hundreds of thousands of prisoners and probationers who are now "under correctional supervision" because of drug offenses would not be rapidly reassimilated into civil society. Eventually, perhaps, but not soon. Once again, the most that the best possible reform can do is to check an undesirable trend. The mistakes already made have consequences that cannot be undone. The criminalized population is in place and no government policy can make it disappear.

The same principle applies even to the dispersed population involved in tort liability. Unlike drug offenders, liability claimants are a population that changes from year to year, as old claims are settled and new ones presented. But the custom of litigating personal injuries whenever there is a chance of financial gain is by now firmly embedded in the national culture. Time was when people only sued about injuries caused by somebody's demonstrable carelessness or malice. But now that the concept of negligence has been expanded to cover all sorts of innocent and well-meaning acts, injured parties are expected to sue their friends, their relatives, their hosts, their employers, their landlords or anyone else with insurance coverage. Even if contingency fees were abolished tomorrow and compulsory arbitration were made universal, there would still be more personal injury claims in this country than in any other, and that would go on for a long, long time.

With respect to the welfare system, the point about incurred costs is too obvious to labor. A baby with no proper family is an incurred cost with a life expectancy of 70-odd years. And society must pay the charges.

These considerations remind us that no program can possibly succeed which starts with a problem and projects an immediate solution. In between that problem and that solution there must be intermediate stages. And it often happens that the early stages of an appropriate program do not resemble the later stages. For example, the first step toward effective welfare reform might be to remove the heavy marginal taxes that are now levied on the earnings of welfare recipients, allowing them to keep all the money they earn until their incomes rise to the poverty level. The later stages of such a program might involve the replacement of means-tested welfare payments by a universal family allowance.

In current practice, proposed social reforms are frequently presented as instant solutions, without any attention to interim stages. This habit of mind is partly responsible for the weak or missing feedback in so many public sector programs. The intended reform may be irrelevant or counterproductive or it may fail because of some overlooked detail, but in the typical episode of this kind, the overseers of the reform do not discover its failure or partial failure in time to take corrective action. The project of reform is conceptualized as a single gesture, not as a sequence of events.

We are reminded again that the requirements of social technology are much the same as those of other commonplace technologies—those that are used in designing a new machine or building it. All the necessities are self-evident—to draw on past experience, set explicit goals, develop a plan, find the appropriate tools and materials, recruit qualified personnel, and do the work in stages.

The only significant difference is that the intended effects of each interim stage of a social project must include specified changes in the incentives of the participants. In the case of service systems, that includes the systems' agents as well as their clients. At any given stage in welfare reform, the incentives of welfare mothers must change or nothing useful happens. And that implies, and indeed requires, corresponding changes in the incentives of the social workers who deal with them.

In most systems, the task of changing the incentives (and thereby the behavior) of the systems' agents is more challenging than that of changing the incentives of their clients. The professionals are better organized, better informed and better able to resist. But it is only wishful thinking to imagine that the behavior of clients can be changed without corresponding modifications in the behavior of the professionals who deal with them. If no one attempts to predict the ways in which incentives and behavior will be affected by a particular reform, it is very likely to achieve results opposite to those intended.

Take, for example, the workfare provisions that have been imposed on the welfare system by federal and state legislation at various times since the 1950s. Welfare mothers typically do not look for work because: (1) they are qualified only for low paying jobs that would give them less income than their present entitlements and (2) they have small children to take care of. Since few of them can be moved directly into the labor force, legislatures quite reasonably provide the alternative of job training. The job training then becomes a legally acceptable substitute for employment and is ritualized as such, somewhat reducing the meager incentives for going to work that were already in the system.

Homeopathic remedies of this kind are the norm in current social policies. Think, for example, of those wonderfully futile cost-containment measures that tell hospitals not to keep patients with a given condition for more than a given number of days, without in any way curtailing their ability to cram more procedures and more charges into each day. Once the mechanism gets working, 6 days of hospitalization cost a good deal more than 12 days used to cost. Such failures of good intentions occur routinely whenever one set of people try to change the behavior of another set of people, and the people whose behavior is being changed react in their own interest. But since these failures occur routinely, they are predictable and potentially manageable.

The foregoing discussion makes it plain that much of social technology is hardly more than codified common sense. But there is, in addition, a considerable body of social science knowledge that can be used to distinguish between workable and unworkable projects, and to predict some of the unintended consequences of workable projects. A great deal is known about how bureaucracies function, what they can and cannot accomplish and how their goals are distorted by their own internal processes. Research on small groups allows us to generalize about the effects of reward and punishment on individual behavior, and the social mediation of those effects. Research in prisons has uncovered the modes of collusion between inmates and guards that enable prisons to function with only intermittent disorder. Research in classrooms has ascertained most of what needs to be known about the learning patterns of children and adolescents. Economic research has answered most of the relevant questions about the causes of poverty. Criminologists have a fair understanding of the etiology of crime. The social patterning of behavior in the health care system is a well-explored area.

Very little of this knowledge has so far been put to use either in the drafting of legislation or in the administration of government programs. No agency has the responsibility of reviewing proposed changes in a public sector system to determine if the intended effects seem credible in the light of what is known about human behavior in general and the activities and relationships peculiar to that system.

To introduce any kind of improvement into an organizational system without continuous monitoring is, of course, irresponsible. But it is the way things are done in the public sector. The only useful short-term feedback provided by most federal and state programs are their appropriation requests which, in the usual case, involve increases over prior appropriations and justifications therefore. It has recently become the practice, at the federal level, to project expenditures several years ahead; almost invariably, these projections are exceeded throughout the life of the program. In theory, the discrepancy between the original projections and the actual costs should be a signal that something has gone wrong and call for corrective action: in practice, long-term budget projections do not pretend to be realistic and are not expected to be taken seriously.

One reason why budgetary projections are so frivolous is that more careful estimates might defeat a politically appealing project. The federal child care system that is currently being installed is a case in point. Being brand new, it is not yet a failing system, but since it disregards the principles of social technology in familiar ways, the chances of failure are excellent, and we may expect to be talking about the crisis of the public child care system in 10 years or so. The few billion dollars of public money that go into child care initially will inevitably raise the price and diminish the availability of the private child care—much of it very informal—that now provides comfort and safety for most of the children of working mothers. The costs of the system will balloon as federally supported child care for the poor raises child care costs across the board, and increases the need for further subsidies, in much the same way that Medicare and Medicaid expanded the aggregate cost of health care.

If anyone undertook to make serious and realistic projections of the eventual monetary costs of the incipient child care program, it would be immediately apparent that the program is unaffordable. Moreover, its basic conception is open to question, since it appears that the only organizations that can operate easily under the system as now planned will be large commercial chains, and the services they provide may, on balance, be inferior to the small-scale services they replace.

At each stage of the child care program there are possible negative effects—profiteering, substandard care, regulatory costs recruitment problems, insurance costs, and of course, the inevitable price escalation. Almost no attention has been given to these easily predictable effects and no one is planning to cope with them when they appear. Yet the identification of potential negative effects is the single most important precaution to take in designing programs in the public sector. It stands at the core of social technology.

Consider drug education. We know that many programs of drug education function as advertising for illegal drugs. Yet it has not been the practice to examine the hundreds of such programs introduced into the public schools in this light and to ask about each particular piece whether its harmful effect might outweigh its beneficial effect. By allowing any presentation about euphoric drugs to qualify as drug education without any estimation of its audience effect, the taxpayers have subsidized a great deal of effective promotion for the drug traffickers they detest.

The one great difference between the objects to which material technology is applied and the people to whom social technology is applied is that the people are more reactive. Regardless of the usefulness of planning in human organizations, it is never reasonable to send down an initial plan and expect it to work its way out to the end. The environment changes. Accidents occur. New factions form. Unexpected benefits appear. Not all unanticipated consequences are negative, but all of them require adjustments in the original plan. In addition to the need for adjustment because elements of the plan have not worked, there are the broader adjustments that need to be made to take new circumstances into account and to adjust objectives to match them. As often as not, the new circumstances are created by the operation of the program itself.

All things considered, the principles of social technology are not complex or difficult to apply, but ever since it became the custom of the country to neglect them in favor of good intentions and symbolic enactments, the effects of legislative and judicial initiatives have been more often harmful than beneficial. The troubles described in the five following chapters stem directly from that neglect.

3 ————————————————————————

HEALTH CARE

CAUSES AND CONSEQUENCES

The American health care system is now being changed, and its future shape is unpredictable, but no one is optimistic enough to think that the consequences of past errors in public policy will be totally overcome. All of the competing reform plans project a reconstructed system that will still be much more expensive per capita than any other in the world and not entirely effective in protecting the general health of the population.

Third party payments without price negotiation are the root cause of the current crisis. Most of the fees paid to health care providers and most of the charges billed by hospitals (about 78 percent of the total) are paid by third parties—government agencies, private insurance companies, managed care plans or self-insured employers.

Under this arrangement, as it developed from the 1960s onward, there was very little price negotiation between third parties and providers and none at all between patients and providers. The patient had no effective bargaining power in his dealings with doctors and hospitals. Patients had no incentive to bargain about the price of a course of treatment and were made to understand that it would be grossly improper to try.

The market for pharmaceutical products was equally peculiar. The people who made the purchase decisions did not pay for the products and often did not know or care what they cost. For a patented prescription product that had no generic substitute, the price was limited only by the manufacturer's imagination.

Adagen, a drug developed by Enzon Inc. of South Plainfield N.J., was the first enzyme replacement therapy to win FDA approval. Adagen treats a rare inherited illness called severe, combined immune deficiency in which the children fail to develop a normal immune system and suffer severe, chronic, infections. Before the drug became available, patients died by age 2. Children now survive with their weekly injection, but each vial of the drug costs $2,200, putting the annual cost between a quarter-million and a half-million dollars, depending on the patient's body weight.[1]

Within the past few years, third party payers *did* begin to bargain about providers' fees and hospital charges. That effort was known as cost-containment. It created a mountain of paperwork—itself very costly—without any perceptible effect on cost escalation. Physicians' fees and hospital charges continued to rise from year to year at more than twice the rate of general inflation. When insurers put ceiling prices on procedures, the providers simply ordered more procedures. When maximum hospital stays were set for particular conditions, the number of charges per day increased accordingly.

THE INCENTIVE STRUCTURE

Third party payment of fees for service generated perverse incentives for everyone in the health care system.

Physicians (together with dentists and other providers) were powerfully motivated to:

— Continually raise their fees
— Find new reasons for patient visits
— Multiply billable procedures
— Overprescribe
— Perform unnecessary surgery
— Overtreat the dying

— Invest in profitable sidelines such as dialysis centers

Hospital administrators were powerfully motivated to:

— Continually raise their charges
— Multiply billable procedures
— "Unbundle" existing procedures to produce more charges
— Extract the maximum profit from terminal cases
— Overinvest in costly equipment
— Turn away indigent patients

Insured patients were powerfully motivated to:

— Accept unnecessary procedures
— Submit to overmedication
— Disregard the cost of elective treatments

Uninsured patients were powerfully motivated to:

— Postpone or avoid necessary treatment
— Seek routine care in emergency rooms

Insurers were powerfully motivated to:

— Improve the risk pool by dropping high-risk claimants
— Reduce coverage by manipulating technicalities
— Intervene in therapeutic decisions
— Shift costs to policyholders
— Engage in fraudulent marketing

Manufacturers and suppliers were powerfully motivated to:

— Set prices unreasonably high
— Promote disposable products
— Invest heavily in marketing to providers
— Conceal evidence of product defects

SYSTEM PERFORMANCE

One look at this gamut of perverse incentives begins to explain why the American health care system, although technically the most advanced in the world and the best equipped, costs a great deal more per capita than the health care system of any other developed nation and gets poorer overall results, as measured by life expectancy, infant mortality and morbidity rates.

The health care systems of these other countries have a variety of organizational structures but none of them involve third party payments of fees set unilaterally by providers. Either the government employs providers and operates hospitals directly, as in Britain; or the government provides full, universal health insurance and sets fees, as in France; or the government provides universal health insurance and negotiates fee schedules, as in Canada; or the entire population is enrolled in managed care organizations, as in Germany. In these countries, every citizen is entitled to comprehensive health care and pays little or nothing for it, while the remuneration of physicians and other health care providers and the budgets of hospitals are either set by public authority or negotiated between parties of comparable bargaining power. These foreign systems are not problem-free, of course. Their costs too have recently been rising, driven by advances in medical technology and the medicalization of conditions such as alcoholism, senility and depression. Some of them have queuing problems, especially for elective surgery. Some of them do not support research and development very well. But all in all they provide adequate levels of care without jeopardizing their respective economies or imposing financial hardships on patients.

None of these foreign systems has a medical malpractice problem like our own. The largest claim in the typical malpractice suit in the United States is for the future medical costs of the injured claimant. In the cases of patients who were permanently disabled by the alleged negligence, the charges for lifelong care in the American system run into huge amounts, further inflated by huge legal costs. The large awards that juries make in some of these suits force (or permit) insurers to set very high premiums for the medical malpractice insurance carried by doctors and hospitals. The threat of even higher premiums and the fear of being sued induce providers to practice "defensive medicine," that is, to order tests and procedures they regard as unnecessary in order to protect themselves against later accusations of negligence. This strategy gives providers an unassailable excuse for increasing the number of billable procedures whenever third party payers set ceilings on fees or limit the length of hospital stays, and it helps to explain the remarkable ineffectiveness of cost-containment efforts so far.

The perverse incentives that loom so large in this field are of relatively recent origin.[2] The private insurance system developed between 1940, when fewer than 10 percent of the U.S. population had any form of health insurance,[3] and 1957, by when about 75 precent had some form of private insurance coverage.[4] With the advent of third party payments, the great price rise began. Total expenditures for medical care, which had remained approximately level from 1920 to 1940, rose, by 293 percent from 1940 to 1957 and by another 300 percent from 1957 to 1970,[5] when the Medicare and Medicaid programs were fully activated. With the bottomless pocket of the federal government available, health care prices and expenditures rose to truly poetic heights. Medicare paid providers $7.1 billion on behalf of patients over 65 in 1970; in 1990, the total exceeded $100 billion, although the population covered had increased by less than two-thirds. A large fraction of Medicare's enormous budget is spent on dying, hospitalized patients for treatment that is often questionable.[6]

Dr. D.J., a 66–year-old physician and confirmed diabetic was admitted to a tertiary care hospital for surgery to repair an aortic aneurysm. [He had a history of severe circulatory problems.] During the operation he suffered two periods of cardiac arrest (stoppage of the heart) and was successfully resuscitated on both occasions, although he was left with some serious brain damage. The operation was technically successful but the patient remained semi-comatose following the procedure. As a result of kidney failure, the patient required daily dialysis. On the third post operative day, he developed severe difficulty in breathing and was placed on a respirator. Severe infections of his lungs required large daily doses of intravenous antibiotics.

Over the next four weeks his wife and family visited him daily. His physicians never mentioned the possibility of discontinuing the "life saving" procedures but left the family with the impression that recovery was possible. It was only after a medical school classmate and long time friend presented the patient's wife with the fact that recovery was extremely unlikely that she suggested that "heroic measures" be ceased. The total period of time in the hospital "prolonging his dying" was five weeks at a cost of four hundred thousand dollars.[7]

The escalation of Medicaid costs from 1970 to 1990 was even steeper, although the effective coverage of the program (the proportion of people in poverty who were included) *fell* during that period. From $2 billion in 1970,[8] the cost of Medicaid went to $115 billion in 1992;[9] by then the program provided coverage to fewer than half of the poor, and not very good coverage either.

The lines begin at sunrise, often before the metal gates have been lifted from a single shop window in Harlem or the Bronx. . . . The street is their waiting room, because there is almost never a place to sit down inside the dilapidated doctors' offices known as "Medicaid mills." Housed in shabby, nondescript store fronts along the most desolate blocks in the city, the clinics are called mills because, for the official New York State reimbursement rate of about $11 per patient visit, doctors grind through dozens of patients in a single hour. Often, exams consist of nothing more than taking the patient's temperature and Medicaid information.[10]

Because Medicaid is partly financed by the states (unlike Medicare), its annual increases of 30 percent or more put enormous pressure on other state-supported activities, especially higher education.

In addition to their intrinsic problems, these programs have been riddled with fraud:

[At a Senate hearing in October 1991] HHS Inspector General Richard P. Kesserow testified about a case in which "over 700 Medicare and Medicaid claims for seat lift chairs had been falsified. . . . " In other cases, the General Accounting Office reported, insurance companies brushed off callers who tried to complain by phone about billings for optical services, X-rays and surgery not received. The companies told them to write a letter to Medicare, the GAO said. . . .

Kesserow said another major problem is that it is easy for unscrupulous operators to obtain from Medicare a "provider number," used by a supplier or medical group to identify them for payment purposes. The system simply does not request enough information and does not check it carefully enough.[11]

Medicare and Medicaid engendered a raft of novel fraudulent practices. "Unbundling" is the artificial inflation of price by chopping up a whole item into pieces that cost far more than the original. For example, "a plastic ostomy costs Medicare $4.50 if purchased as a single item, but up to $12.50 if its three component parts are purchased." Vendors practice "variable pricing" so that, "payment for one type of knee-ankle-foot brace varies from $375 to $16." Finally, there is "carrier shopping" which works like this: When a Medicare insurance carrier is paying much more for a particular item in one region than in others, the supplier sets up a business front in the higher-paying region and bills all of his sales from there.[12] But simple overpricing remains as the preferred—and legal—method of bilking health insurers. In January 1993, the General Accounting Office classified the entire Medicare program as "high risk," alleging that the program loses billions of dollars to fraud and that its payment policies encourage abuse and excessive charges by hospitals, doctors, laboratories and clinics.[13]

Medicare has often paid charges submitted by nonprofit hospitals for such items as the air travel of executives' wives, box seats at football games, "educational" trips to China, club memberships, limousine rentals and the other appurtenances of corporate chic. GAO investigations in the 1980s uncovered overcharges to Medicare by hundreds of hospitals, but throughout that decade, only one hospital was compelled to make restitution.[14]

An even more costly problem was the "DRG creep" that appeared in hospital accounts after Medicare's 1983 establishment of ceiling payments to hospitals for Diagnosis Related Groups (DRG)—its prime method of hospital cost containment. The creep in question consisted of electing the DRG with a higher ceiling in the hundreds of thousands of cases where alternative diagnoses are possible. Computer programs were even devised to make this procedure routine. The most interesting thing about DRG creep is that it was foreseen before the system was ever introduced—one of the rare instances in which the perverse incentive generated by a federal program did not appear unexpectedly but was visible in advance.[15]

Another relatively new practice that verges on fraud is the ownership by doctors of commercial diagnostic and treatment facilities to which they refer their unknowing patients. The editor of the *New England Journal of Medicine* described this situation to a congressional committee in 1989:

At the present time, there are thousands of U.S. doctors—and their numbers are increasing rapidly—who are referring their patients to health-care facilities and services which are outside of their offices and independent of their own practices, but in which they have a financial interest....There are all sorts of diagnostic laboratories, physical therapy centers, home health services, et cetera, et cetera.

Now, many of these ventures are very profitable, producing dividends for the participating physicians well in excess of ordinary investments. A few of them may be providing patients with services that might not otherwise be conveniently available, especially in small communities.

But on balance, most of these facilities are located in areas where they are competing with many others.... There are many duplicating facilities nearby, and I believe they are bad for the public and unethical for the profession.[16]

The predatory pricing of health care has effects that extend beyond the operating problems of the public and private insurance plans.

One primary effect is that the portion of the health care bill paid directly by individuals gets more costly along with the portion paid by third parties, which partly nullifies the protective function of health insurance. The people who were over 65 in 1990, although covered by Medicare, paid proportionately more of their own incomes for health care than the people who were over 65 before Medicare was introduced in 1968. A fully insured family could be ruined anyhow by the medical expenses of a protracted illness. At the same time, the cost of individual insurance coverage soared out of the reach of most of the people who were not eligible for Medicare, Medicaid or employer-paid coverage. According to an official estimate, about 34 million Americans had no health insurance at all in 1989;[17] about a third of them were children.[18] Another 100 million were only partially protected. The sale of "Medigap" policies to plug the holes in Medicare coverage became a thriving industry; but few of these policies offered comprehensive coverage and many of them were tinged with fraud. The long-term care policies that purported to supplement Medicaid were even worse. According to a 1991 review by a consumer organization:

Insurance companies are pushing consumers to buy long-term-care policies. So are government officials eager to cut Medicaid spending. The evidence suggests they are succeeding. More than 1.5 million policies have been sold to date. . . . But behind the sales statistics are signs of serious trouble. . . . Poorly trained and sometimes unscrupulous agents are seriously misleading buyers about the terms, benefits and limitations of their coverage. . . . The policies themselves. . . . still have significant shortcomings. Among the traps awaiting consumers: tricky provisions in the way policies are written; the potential for unaffordably large increases; uncertainty about whether claims will be paid; and confounding policy language.[19]

Even when individuals not covered by group plans were willing and able to buy health insurance, they were often unable to obtain it. Insurance companies worked very hard to improve their risk pools by identifying and excluding those applicants who were most likely to become claimants, and by dropping policyholders with chronic conditions. One advocacy group estimated in 1991 that 81 million Americans under the age of 65 had conditions (such as arthritis and diabetes) that might induce insurers to deny or withdraw individual coverage, or to raise individual premiums.[20]

Moreover, insurers have often denied claims by policyholders on the ground that they were not informed of a pre-existing condition. When employers elected to be self-insured, they might be even less generous:

The case involves a small Houston company that shifted its health coverage from a group plan offered by an insurance carrier to self-insurance. When it did so, the company reduced several benefits, including payments for AIDS-related illness, which were dropped from $1 million to $5,000.[21]

The unavailability of individual health insurance at reasonable cost put the unemployed in a medical limbo.[22] People who got sick or were injured while between jobs were in many cases forced to choose between foregoing treatment or going bankrupt.

To the roster of 35 million uninsured Americans, add Rosemarie Mingus. Until last week, the former Pan Am purser and her family were covered by one of the best health policies in the nation. Now, they have nothing. . . . "This is a nightmare," said Mingus, who is now scrambling to find alternative insurance or a health maintenance organization that will accept her husband and two children at rates they can afford. "To have kids and not have health insurance," she said, "is one of the most frightening things you can imagine."[23]

The number of active workers and their dependents who were uninsured or inadequately insured increased by leaps and bounds after 1985 as employers struggled with the continuous escalation of health premiums, which more than doubled between 1980 and 1987, and more than doubled again between 1987 and 1992. It became standard practice for large firms to deny health benefits to temporary, part-time and contract employees. Some of them did not provide coverage for new employees until after a probationary period; others screened job applicants for health risks. Nearly all firms shifted some of the cost of dependent coverage to employees and concurrently increased the deductible and co-insurance amounts payable by employees. As of 1990, the majority of small employers no longer provided any health benefits at all.[24]

Retiree health benefits were particularly at risk. The bitter Pittston Coal strike of 1989 was caused in part by the company's decision to cancel health benefits for disabled and retired miners. Spokesmen for General Motors alleged that the cost of retiree health insurance added a penalty of $500 to every car they produced, and put them at a competitive disadvantage with transplanted Japanese automakers who were too new to have retirees. Most large firms actively whittled away at the health benefits of past retirees while reducing the entitlements of future retirees.[25] Some went further and phased out retiree health benefits altogether. In announcing such a phase-out for their 46,000 retired employees, Unisys and General Dynamics expressed the hope that some national plan would eventually rescue these medical orphans.[26]

Health benefits became for some years the principal issue in the negotiation of labor contracts. Unions saw the curtailment of health benefits as the most serious economic risk, aside from unemployment, facing their members. Firms saw the ever-increasing cost of health benefits as a threat to their profitability and survival.

The situation got clean out of hand.

Spokesmen for the existing system vehemently denied that the extraordinary inflation of health care costs between 1970 and 1990 had anything to do with the extraordinary profit opportunities that

Medicare and Medicaid gave to providers. They ascribed it instead to the aging of the population, the progress of medical technology and insatiable consumer demand for health services. But the relevant numbers favor the simpler explanation. Given the perverse incentive to raise their fees continually and send the bill to the government, the providers obliged.

The combined influence of the aging population, the growth of consumer demand and the progress of medical technology on the medical price structure seems rather modest compared to the influence of providers in kiting prices and multiplying procedures.

Between 1960 and 1991, the total U.S. population over age 65 grew by 90 percent[27] while the cost of their health care, in constant dollars, increased by more than 1,500 percent. The per person number of office visits to doctors by persons over 65 has been approximately level since 1975, the first year in which that information was collected by survey.[28] Hospital utilization *declined* after 1970.[29] There is no evidence at all of recent growth in the aggregate consumer demand for health care.

The progress of medical technology is less easily dismissed as a cost-raising factor, but in other industries, the introduction of new technology tends to lower costs, not raise them. Better diagnostic instruments, improved medications and simplified surgical procedures should have made the treatment of many conditions easier and cheaper if the health care system had not been so well organized to prevent price reductions. On the other hand, some extraordinarily expensive procedures became widely available during the past two decades—organ transplants, open heart operations, kidney dialysis, the rescue of premature infants, heroic treatment of the dying and drug therapy for AIDS.

The perverse incentive to overtreat, in a system where overtreatment is always financially rewarding to providers, has severe— sometimes life-threatening—consequences for patients. Although the medical literature on unnecessary surgery is very sparse, there are indications of large-scale abuse. The 1985 Senate hearing on unnecessary surgery on the elderly elicited evidence that the number of operations of every type performed on patients over 65 rose disproportionately after the introduction of Medicare. For example, heart catheterization, which had been about equally frequent for patients under and over 65 before Medicare became three times as frequent for elderly patients afterwards. All of the commoner operations—coronary bypasses, gallbladder removals, hysterectomies, prostatectomies, D&Cs—are performed at a much higher rate in the United States than anywhere else in the world. About 24 percent of all United States births are now cesarean—four times as many as in 1971.[30]

Like many couples, Ginny and Peter looked forward and planned for a natural delivery of their first baby. They took Lamaze classes and thought about the first happy moment they would share as a family. But it didn't work out quite the way they planned. Ginny started feeling contractions on a Thursday evening, went to the hospital immediately, and labored there for 24 hours. At eight o'clock on Friday night, her doctor decided that he wanted to do a caesarean section. "He said, 'this baby is never going to come out,' " remembers Ginny. "We asked for more time but he said it might be risking the baby's health."[31]

The doctor's perverse incentives were cumulative in this case. He was paid more for the cesarean than for a vaginal birth, he saved a night's sleep and he reduced the risk of an eventual malpractice suit if the baby were defective.

COST GAMES

The distress of Ginny and Peter was probably augmented by having to pay a good part of the extra cost of the operation they did not want. As the pressure of rising costs on third party payers became intolerable, they found a thousand ways of shifting them. The authors of the most comprehensive recent study of health care financing[32] identified cost-shifting as the system's most serious problem. It took various forms.[33] According to a *Wall Street Journal* article in 1988, "Some hospitals and doctors are submitting inflated bills to traditional corporate health plans to offset cutbacks in payments from Medicare and managed-care plans."[34] A 1989 study of Colorado hospitals estimated that the average hospital bill included $2,290 of shifted costs. Those costs were attributable to the unavoidable treatment of the indigent and uninsured; bad debts; cuts in Medicare, Medicaid, and insurance entitlements; and special prices negotiated with hospitals by managed-care plans.

The prime targets of cost-shifting were large corporate employers, especially those who were self-insured. They in turn found ways to shift costs to their employees and pensioners.

As long as cost-shifting was possible, cost-containment efforts in one sector of the health care system merely raised the burden on other sectors, without much effect on the revenues of providers.

In still another case, Blue Cross terminated home nursing care for a patient suffering from a long-term ailment who had been coping at home for many years. The patients, Blue Cross decided, should go into a nursing home. But wouldn't that be far more expensive? Of course—but in a nursing home, Medicaid pays and not Blue Cross.[35]

Beginning around 1980, all of the third party payers—Medicare, Medicaid, Blue Cross/Blue Shield, hundreds of other private insurers, self-insured employers and managed-care organizations—introduced cost-containment measures. They included the requirement of a second opinion prior to elective surgery, maximum hospital stays for each diagnosed condition, limited reimbursement for office visits and procedures, increased deductibles and co-payments charged to patients, tightened eligibility requirements, and the rejection of as many claims as possible on technicalities.

Some of these measures were temporarily effective. The second opinion requirement dramatically reduced the number of coronary bypass operations for a time, without any adverse effect on patient mortality,[36] but as second opinions became institutionalized, the effect wore off; by 1990, the second opinion had become a meaningless formality in most cases. The limits on hospital stays sent many patients home while they were still very sick but had no appreciable effect on costs; hospitals learned to cram more procedures and charges into fewer days. Many of the physicians who accepted limited reimbursement for office visits were able to make up the difference by charging for tests and supplementary procedures; others billed their patients for a percentage over the official fee.

The cost of routine treatment for patients without third party coverage, or with inadequate coverage, were shifted to the providers of last resort—the emergency rooms of public hospitals. For millions of Americans, the emergency room took the place of the private physician whose services they could no longer afford. The crowding of these facilities by patients seeking routine treatment reduced their ability to handle genuine emergencies. But the demand being nearly limitless, any attempt to alleviate crowding, or reduce waiting times, only attracted more customers.

Patients with ear infections or other easily treated conditions continually pack emergency rooms that look and smell like kennels. Facilities designed to handle about 20 patients often hold 100. Patients wait for hours or days on pallets, wrapped in hospital gowns with their possessions packed into plastic bags. Interminable waits have become so routine that hospitals provide food service for the emergency rooms. For those who need to use bedpans, privacy is beyond hope.[37]

The cost of treating a nonemergency condition in an emergency room is generally much higher than it would be in a doctor's office, but here it is the patient who succeeds in cost-shifting.

THE SEARCH FOR SOLUTIONS

In the early 1990s, it was a truism that the health care system needed drastic reform, but most of the proposals put before the public and debated in Congress did not directly address the overpricing of medical services and products, the overtreatment of patients, or the overstaffing and overequipping of hospitals—all driven by simple but perverse monetary incentives. Some of the proposals for universal, comprehensive health insurance would pump more money into the system without changing the incentive structure that created the existing problem. The likely result would be another round of frantic cost escalation, like that which followed the introduction of Medicare. More sophisticated plans, such as the one sent to Congress by President Clinton in November 1993, relied on the bargaining power of large managed-care organizations and competition among them, combined with a cap on health insurance premiums, to check the escalation of medical and pharmaceutical prices, without much expectation of bringing them down to a reasonable level.

Admittedly, past errors limit the possibilities of reform. Physicians and dentists have become accustomed to very high incomes. They will not gracefully submit to having them reduced. Thousands of them have invested in profit-making diagnostic and treatment facilities to which they refer their patients. They are not about to divest. Hospitals are no longer able to function without duplicative staff and equipment. Pharmaceutical manufacturers and medical suppliers are not likely to take to competitive pricing after so many happy years of charging whatever their captive markets would bear. Even under the most favorable scenario, the U.S. health care system will continue to be the most expensive in the world for the foreseeable future.

A viable reform of the system should do the following things:

— Make adequate health care available to every resident of the United States
— Simplify the Byzantine structure of medical accounting
— Remove the perverse incentives that make it advantageous for providers to overtreat and overcharge
— Reduce the inflation of health care costs to approximately the general rate of inflation

There is no conceivable way these goals can be met in the existing system, with all the perverse incentives that are built into it. To find alternatives, we need only look at the health care systems of the other developed countries, all of which take better care of their people at lower cost with much less wear and tear.

There are three leading models.

The first model is a national health service, operated by the government, with providers on salary. Treatment is free, and costs are met out of public revenues. The British example is the best known. There is a small but prosperous private sector that caters to patients who want more personalized service and are willing to pay for it. By most accounts, the system works well; it gets very favorable ratings in British opinion surveys. But the probability that a similar system might be adopted in the United States is close to zero. It would have to overcome the nearly unanimous opposition of health care professionals and the average citizen's reasonable distrust of the government's managerial ability.

The second model is a system of universal, mandatory health insurance, like that of Canada—commonly called the "single-payer plan." There are no significant user fees. Coverage is comprehensive and available to all residents without discrimination. The provincial governments are the sole payers. They negotiate fees and charges with providers. Providers are able to increase their incomes by treating more patients; patients have a freer choice of providers than under the current U.S. system. When the Canadian system was developing in the late 1960s, Canada spent a slightly higher percentage of GNP on health care than the United States. Although both percentages rose in the two following decades, Canadian expenditures rose much less. Nearly all the relevant numbers now favor Canada. Life expectancy is slightly higher, and infant mortality is substantially lower, the proportion of primary care physicians is much higher, and the ratios of hospital beds and admissions to the population are almost identical, but the average length of stay by Canadian patients is nearly twice as long. The relative number of coronary bypass operations performed in Canada is more than two-thirds less. Physician overhead as a percent of revenue is more than a third less. Malpractice premiums are 85 percent lower than in the United States![38]

The most common criticism of the Canadian system is that it involves considerable queuing for diagnostic procedures and elective surgery. On the other hand, there appears to be less queuing in Canada than currently in the United States for office appointments with specialists.

The Canadian system retains a number of perverse incentives that are reflected in the recent growth of its budget. As in the United States, physicians and other providers stand to gain when they increase the number of procedures in a patient visit. The difference is that they have less latitude to raise their charges. Canadian hospitals stand to gain by prolonging patient stays beyond what is clinically necessary and the numbers suggest that they do so.

The Canadian plan might well be workable south of the border. Its proponents point to the cultural similarity between the two countries and the close resemblance of their medical institutions. The possibility of adopting the Canadian system was discussed in federal publications[39] well before it gathered adherents in Congress. One American state, Hawaii, actually operates a variant of the Canadian system.

But the model that seems to have guided the thinking of the Clinton Commission is German rather than Canadian. The German health care system has only recently begun to attract attention in this country.[40] In 1977 the Federal Republic adopted an explicit national policy that aimed to prevent any further increases in the health sector's share of gross national product and succeeded in doing so. That result was achieved without any perceptible reduction in the quality of care. Today's complex system has evolved over a long period of time beginning with Bismarckian social insurance measures introduced in the 1880s, but the removal of perverse incentives is a recent, deliberate accomplishment.

The German system provides comprehensive health care to the entire population (even to temporary residents and tourists) at virtually no personal cost, although there are co-payments for visits to spas and for some kinds of dental work. The heart of the system is a distinction between ambulatory care physicians, who charge fees for their services, and hospital physicians and surgeons, who are salaried. The recipients of health services are represented by nearly 1,200 sickness funds, supported by matching contributions from employed persons and their employers. The providers are represented by regional medical associations and hospital boards. All medical bills are paid by the sickness funds to the medical associations, which reimburse their members for the services they have rendered to patients. The per diem charges of hospitals are also paid through the sickness funds. Fees and charges are renegotiated annually by collective bargaining between the sickness funds and the providers' representatives, under the oversight of the federal government, which also subsidizes the sickness fund memberships of retired and unemployed persons and others outside the labor force. Hospital patients incur a flat per diem charge, regardless of condition or treatment. The capital costs of hospital construction and equipment are met out of public funds and do not enter into hospital budgets. The annual renegotiation of medical fees and hospital charges between each sickness fund and its nearby providers is constrained by guidelines that limit cost increases to the increase of employer-employee contributions. Since the percentage contributed by employers and employees is held approximately constant by legislative mandate, sickness fund budgets cannot rise faster than the earnings of their members. Pharmaceutical manufacturers are subject to strict price controls.

Germany currently provides superb health care for its entire population at about half the per capita cost of health care in the United States.

There are some perverse incentives left in the German system. Patients are tempted to overutilize medical and hospital services that cost them nothing. If Iglehart's (1991) figures are correct, Germans visit their doctors more often than Americans do and their average hospital stays are much longer. Ambulatory physicians have incentives to raise their incomes by attracting more patients and encouraging more visits. Hospitals have an incentive to prolong patient stays in order to maximize their revenue from per diem charges. But these efforts are self-limiting since any aggregate increase in patient visits or hospital days exerts a downward pressure on physicians' fees and hospital charges. Since 1977, when this form of cost-containment was introduced, the average income of physicians has indeed declined in relative terms, although it is still very high compared to that of the average worker.

The German system removes, or rather reverses, the perverse incentives for unnecessary surgery and the overtreatment of dying patients that loom so large in our own hospitals, since German hospitals do not gain any additional revenue from operations or other costly procedures. Theoretically, this reversed incentive might raise the danger of undertreatment but this does not seem to be a significant problem. Nor are there many complaints about queuing. The sickness funds and the regional medical associations, which handle all of the billings of the populations they represent, are admirably placed to review clinical performance and continually do so. The imbalances that develop between resources and needs enter the agenda of the annual negotiations.

This system, despite its obvious advantages, is not entirely suitable for the United States. The German sickness funds have a long history, dating back to 1911. It would probably be impossible to create their equivalents in the short term. Other important features of the German system are the separation of ambulatory care practice from hospital practice and the salaried status of hospital staff. Those features too are difficult to visualize in this country, where ambulatory and hospital care are closely interwoven, surgeons are politically influential and even the faculties of medical schools are increasingly supported by patient fees.[41]

The key features of the German system that might be adapted to American conditions are: (1) universal coverage, (2) the insulation of patients from any direct financial involvement with doctors and hospitals, (3) a collective bargaining process between patient and provider associations of approximately equal strength; (4) the local negotiation of fees and charges under national guidelines, (5) the financing of health care primarily from payroll contributions and (6) the adoption of a national policy against further increases in the health care share of the economy.

Most of the national health care plans that are currently under discussion include some but not all of the foregoing elements. They envisage a large-scale shift to managed-care plans, whereby individuals and families obtain comprehensive health service from a group of providers for an annual payment. For persons in the labor force and their families, the payments might be made either by employers or by the employees themselves. For those not otherwise covered, the government would pick up the tab.

That would assure adequate health care for the entire population if payments and services are the same for all beneficiaries. Otherwise, a tier of inferior service would surely develop for the special benefit of the poor, as has happened with Medicaid.

These plans do not represent a radical departure from existing practice in some corners of the American health care system. But they would require fundamental changes in the roles of third party payers. Their attempts to contain costs piecemeal, without setting aggregate limits on medical and hospital charges, have led to their constant, clumsy interference in the clinical management of cases; their insensitivity to the hardships of patients; and their mountains of pointless paperwork.

The first step in returning to a workable system is the national policy that asserts a universal right to comprehensive health care. The second and more difficult step is the imposition of limits on aggregate spending that cannot be evaded by cost-shifting but will be met, when necessary, by downward adjustments in medical fees, hospital charges and supplier prices. If those budgetary limits were set so as to hold health care costs at their current percentage of the gross domestic product, the United States would continue to have the most lavishly financed health care in the world but the pain and suffering caused by it would be considerably reduced.

A number of states—Hawaii, Minnesota, Oregon—have already established some form of universal health insurance. Hawaii has a variant of the single-payer plan. Minnesota is a specially interesting case because it had a relatively small uninsured population and an exceedingly large and influential medical establishment. Its plan calls for compulsory insurance coverage of all employed workers and their families, with the state paying the premium for unemployed persons ineligible for Medicaid or Medicare. Insurance companies are not allowed to withdraw coverage from individuals suffering from AIDS or other expensive conditions, or to adjust premiums to individual risks. The state finances its contribution to the plan by a 2 percent tax on medical and hospital services. Cost control is envisaged but deferred; the problem is to be studied by a commission.

The Oregon plan is, so far, unique in setting up a table of medical priorities and setting an aggregate limit on what the state pays for a program that includes Medicaid but goes beyond it to cover the uninsured poor. Coverage is allowed for 587 conditions but denied for 121 others, including some very expensive ones: liver transplants for alcoholic cirrhosis, intensive treatment of end-stage HIV disease and of extremely premature infants.

It has been easier for states to extend health insurance coverage to the uninsured than to set a limit on aggregate health expenditures. For the nation as a whole, the challenge is formidable, since the two major objectives of reform—to make basic health services available to the uninsured and inadequately insured, and to prevent the aggregate bill from taking a still greater share of national income—are potentially incompatible. It will be difficult enough to enact any effective limitation of medical fees, hospital charges and pharmaceutical prices. A successful rollback is almost unimaginable.

NOTES

1. Larry Thompson, "The High Cost of Rare Diseases," *Washington Post Health* (June 25, 1991): 10–13.

2. For a succinct account of how it developed, see Joseph Califano, *America's Health Care Revolution: Who Lives? Who Dies? Who Pays?* (New York: Random House, 1986).

3. U.S. Bureau of the Census, *Historical Statistics of the United States: Colonial Times to 1970,* Series G 440 (Washington, DC: GPO, 1975).

4. *Statistical Abstract of the United States 1954* (hereafter *SAUS*), Tables 604, 605.

5. *SAUS93,* Table 156.

6. Kenneth R. Crispell and Carlos P. Gomez, "Proper Care for the Dying: A Critical Public Issue," *Journal of Medical Ethics* 13 (1987): 74–80.

7. Ibid., 75.

8. *SAUS79,* Table 143.

9. Kaiser Committee on Medicaid (1991).

10. Michael Specter, "Medicaid's Malady," *Washington Post* (July 8, 1991): A1, A8.

11. Spencer Rich, "Medicare Fraud, Lax Investigations Cost Hundreds of Millions, Hill Told," *Washington Post* (October 3, 1991): A21.

12. Hilary Stout, "U.S. Health Officials Offer Regulations to Curb Abuses by Equipment Suppliers," *Wall Street Journal* (November 4, 1991): B4.

13. Dana Priest, "Waste and Fraud Rampant in Medicare, GAO Charges," *Washington Post* (January 8, 1993): A2.

14. Walt Bogdanich, *The Great White Lie: How America's Hospitals Betray our Trust and Endanger our Lives* (New York: Simon and Schuster, 1991), chapters 7 and 8.

15. Donald W. Simborg, M.D., "DRG Creep: A New Hospital-Acquired Disease," *New England Journal of Medicine* 304, no. 26 (June 25, 1981): 1602–1604.

16. U.S. Congress, House, Committee on Ways and Means, *Issues Related to Physical "Self-Referrals,"* Serial 101–58 (1989): 30–31, testimony of Arnold S. Relman, M.D.

17. National Center for Health Statistics, *Health Insurance and Medical Care: Health of Our Nation's Children, United States, 1988,* Advance Data No. 188 (1990); National Center for Health Statistics, *Characteristics of Persons With and Without Health Care Coverage, United States, 1989,* Advance Data No. 201 (1991).

18. Center for Health Statistics: *Health Insurance* and *Characteristics of Persons.*

19. *Consumer Reports* (June 1991): 425.

20. Citizen Action, quoted by Associated Press (June 10, 1991).

21. Robert Kuttner, "Our Unraveling Health Care System," *Washington Post* (December 10, 1991): A21.

22. See U.S. General Accounting Office, *Health Insurance: Bibliography of Studies on Health Benefits for the Uninsured,* GAO/HRD-89–27FS (February 1989).

23. William Booth, "Hard Times Fray Health Safety Net," *Washington Post* (December 19, 1991): A1, A30.

24. U.S. General Accounting Office, *Health Insurance: Cost Increases Lead to Coverage Limitations and Cost Shifting*, GAO/HRD-90-68 (May 1990).

25. Ibid.

26. Dean C. Coddington, David J. Keen, Keith D. Moore and Richard L. Clarke, *The Crisis in Health Care* (San Francisco: Jossey-Bass, 1990), pp. 103.

27. *SAUS91*, Table 13, and *SAUS93*, Table 14.

28. National Center for Health Statistics, *National Ambulatory Medical Care Survey, 1989*, Advance Data No. 203 (1991): Figure 3.

29. *SAUS92*, Table 173.

30. In 1970 there were 5.5 cesarean section deliveries per 100 total deliveries. By 1989, this had risen to 23.8 cesareans per 100 births, an increase of 433 percent. See *SAUS92*, Table 86.

31. Janice Kaplan, "Do Caesareans Save Lives?" *Parents* (January 1988): 84–86ff.

32. Coddington et al., *Crisis in Health Care*.

33. U.S. GAO, *Health Insurance* (May 1990).

34. Glenn Ruffenach, "Health Insurance Premiums to Soar in '89," *Wall Street Journal* (October 25, 1988): B1.

35. Robert Kuttner, "Health Care Horrors," *Washington Post* (August 2, 1991): A25.

36. U.S. Congress, Senate, Special Committee on Aging, *Unnecessary Surgery: Double Jeopardy for Older Americans*, GPO Serial No. 99-1 (1985).

37. *Boston Globe* (March 1, 1990): 9.

38. Suzi Borgo, "Health Care Trends in the United States and Canada," unpublished seminar paper, University of Virginia, 1991.

39. U.S. General Accounting Office, *Canadian Health Insurance: Lessons for the United States*, GAO/HRD-91-90, 1991.

40. John K. Iglehart "Health Policy Report: Germany's Health Care System," *New England Journal of Medicine* 324, no. 7 (1991): 503–508, and 324, no. 24 (1991): 1750–1756.

41. Dolores Burke, *Physicians in the Academic Marketplace* (Westport, CT: Greenwood Press, 1991).

4

THE PUBLIC SCHOOLS

CAUSES AND CONSEQUENCES

Technological backwardness and outmoded organization are the root causes of perverse incentives in U.S. public schools. Almost all teaching is done with the methods and equipment of the nineteenth century, and the classroom is organized to fit the conditions and the people of a bygone time. It is a wonder that the system works at all.

The 84,000 public schools that offer free instruction from kindergarten through high school spend about $200 billion annually. Like the other failing systems, this one suffers from continuous cost escalation. In constant dollars, school expenditures increased by 203 percent between 1965 and 1991, but the capacity of the system did not increase at all. Enrollment varied from year to year but remained in the range between 39 million and 46 million (42 million in 1991), while the number of teachers increased from 1.7 million to 2.5 million.[1] The system is labor-intensive and capital-poor. Most of the money goes to salaries and wages. The capital investment per worker is exceedingly low.

Education is tied with social work as the most labor-intensive business in the economy, with labor costs equal to 93 percent of output value—compared with 54 percent for all private business. . . . Education has by far the lowest level of capital investment of any major industry, with only $1000 per employee. The average for the U.S. economy as a whole is about $50,000 of capital investment per job; in some high-tech industries it is $300,000 or more.[2]

This system has fewer defenders than any of the others discussed in this book. The chorus of criticism and condemnation swells louder with each passing year. The crisis in public education has been the subject of a vast literature, innumerable conferences and a convocation of all fifty governors called by then-President Bush. Teachers and their organizations are as critical of the system as everyone else. Public opinion is virtually unanimous about the need for drastic reforms but there is no consensus about what the reforms should be.

Paradoxically, the majority of American parents are satisfied with the public schools their own children attend.[3] But that does not shake their conviction that the larger system of public education is in desperate condition.

The commonly cited problems are (1) the inability of U.S. public schools to teach their pupils as much as the schools in any other developed country, (2) the paucity of homework and concentrated study, (3) the "functional illiteracy" of some high school graduates, (4) excessive dropouts from high school, (5) the inferior academic qualifications of teachers compared to other college-educated workers, (6) the substandard preparation of teachers in specific subjects, especially mathematics and science, (7) the inferior earnings of teachers compared to other college-educated workers, (8) the disorder, verging on anarchy, that prevails in many schools, (9) the perpetuation of social inequalities between schools by means of unequal local funding and (10) the combination of ever-rising cost and stable or declining performance.

To make matters worse, there is the embarrassing comparison that cannot be avoided between the public schools and the competing private sector of Catholic schools, other religious schools, secular day schools and boarding schools. The private schools enroll about 14 percent of the elementary school population and 7 percent of the high school population.[4] As a group they spend significantly less per pupil but their academic outcomes are better, and they and their teachers are more respected by their constituencies.[5] These differences can be explained away by pointing to the greater involvement of parents and the tighter classroom discipline in the private schools, but that only highlights the problem.

THE INCENTIVE STRUCTURE

In the existing system, teachers in the public schools are powerfully motivated to:

— Restrict the progress of a class through a subject to the pace of the slowest students
— Assign a minimum of homework
— Promote and graduate nonachieving students
— Cover for incompetent colleagues
— Resist innovation

Pupils are powerfully motivated to:

— Refrain from any unusual scholarly effort that might annoy their peers
— Do a minimum of homework and concentrated study
— Avoid difficult subjects
— Treat teachers as adversaries

SYSTEM PERFORMANCE

Until the 1970s, the aggregate output of the public schools had been steadily increasing for longer than anyone could remember. The proportion of adolescents who graduated from high school rose from 2 percent in 1870 to 9 percent in 1910 to 29 percent in 1930 to 76 percent in 1975. Then it stopped rising and declined a bit.[6]

The interruption of productivity growth was accompanied by the cessation of quality improvement. Average SAT scores declined for a while and then leveled off. Tests of subject proficiency at various grade levels showed negligible progress after 1973.[7]

While American education stagnated, other countries were racing ahead. In a 1988 international comparison of mathematical and science proficiency, American 13–year olds trailed their counterparts in such places as Ireland and Korea. In a larger study three years later that included 15 nations, they were again near the bottom of the list, below Slovenia and barely edging out Jordan.[8] Another 1992 study, involving 18 countries, showed similar results.[9] Although there are some recent, encouraging signs—high school dropout rates fell in the 1980s, a rising proportion of high school seniors enrolled in basic subjects—there is broad agreement that American youth are inadequately educated and that an "education deficit" impairs the quality of the labor force and the competitiveness of U.S. industry.[10]

There can be no serious question that the productivity of the American public school system is low compared to that of competing foreign systems. But there is not much evidence of a real decline in productivity. The famous drop in SAT scores during the 1970s was small and easily explained by the inclusion of less qualified students in the college applicant pool. What seems to have happened is that the public schools stagnated, clinging to archaic work methods, antiquated equipment and outmoded practices, while foreign systems advanced. Nothing in our society looks, smells and sounds more old-fashioned than an elementary school in a middle-sized city. The curriculum, the organizational chart, the division of labor and the daily routine are much as they were in 1920.

But the world outside has not stood still since 1920 or even since 1960. Koreans and Slovenians began to educate their children for full participation in an industrial society. Most of the mothers of U.S. children left home for the workplace, automatically reducing the encouragement they could give to their children's school work. More and more U.S. children lived in families without fathers, or with unsympathetic stepfathers. When teachers were no longer able to count on parental supervision of homework, they stopped assigning it. When parents were unwilling or unable to reinforce school discipline, teachers relaxed their efforts to maintain order.

Something similar happened with regard to teacher qualifications. The teachers' colleges of the 1990s undoubtedly provide better training than the normal schools of the 1920s. But the normal school graduate of the 1920s was a highly educated professional compared to the average parent of that era, who had left school before finishing the eighth grade, while today's teacher faces an average parent who has had more than a year of college.

Knowledge itself has undergone a transformation. In 1920, any literate person could learn enough in a few weeks of hard study to teach a high school course in physics or social studies. When that is attempted today, the results are ludicrous. It is commonplace for high school students to be badly misinformed about nuclear fission or the business cycle by teachers who do not know the subjects they teach.

The legacy of the normal school to schools and colleges of education was an emphasis on the study of pedagogical methods that tends to displace specialization in substantive fields. This made sense in the days when the students who entered normal schools were already better educated than most of the population and the material they were to teach was simpler and less changeable. Moreover, the course of study in the normal school was typically brief. Today's colleges of education must stretch the thin body of positive knowledge about pedagogy to fit a two- or four- or five-year format. This unnourishing curriculum is not attractive to superior applicants, and one result is that students majoring in education have lower than average scores on tests of scholastic aptitude.[11] Another result is that most education graduates are more or less unqualified to teach science, mathematics or social studies because they do not have enough background in those dynamic fields to keep up with new developments. The problem has not gone unnoticed, of course, and numerous reforms have been suggested and tried; the most successful appears to be the offer of a quick and easy master's degree in teaching to liberal arts graduates. But the problem persists. Almost all public school systems refuse to license teachers who lack a degree in education. The majority of university professors would not be eligible to teach their subjects in a public high school. This practice partly accounts for the superior performance of the private schools, whose teachers have degrees in substantive fields but lack the education credentials that would entitle them to the higher salaries paid by the public schools. No one seriously believes that their teaching is the worse for that lack.

The structure of social control is something else that has changed in the outside world while the classroom stood still. In recent decades, personal authority of all kinds has been declining in Western societies,[12] including the general authority of adults over children and adolescents. Teachers have less authority over their pupils in much the same way that employers have less authority over their employees and priests have less authority over their parishioners. Authoritarian control in personal interaction has largely gone out of style. But while factories and churches have adapted to this cultural shift, the schools have not. The balance of power in today's classrooms is so unstable that maintaining order often takes priority over instruction. The instability of control is obvious in chaotic inner-city schools, but it is also a factor in small town high schools with middle-income students. A teacher in such a school shares a moment with us:

A crescendo of chairs sliding, foot scraping, book shuffling, and talking at the end of the hall. A class full of seniors streams through Judy Bickel's doorway. I check my watch: 8:31. Six minutes to go. Why is Judy letting these kids out six minutes early. This disorder must be contained. I think like a cop. This commotion will disrupt every class on the hallway; students will look at watches, close books, begin conversations; dramatic climaxes; teachers will yell at kids for being rude; kids will think teachers are jerks for being too demanding; assignments will be missed. This disorder must be contained. I think like a teacher. I rise and jog towards the mob.
    "Hey guys, how come you're out in the hall? It's only eight thirty-one."
    "The sub let us out early."
    "Well, listen, you wanna keep the noise down a little, please?"
    "Mumble yea mumble no problem mumble."
    "And you wanna turn off the stereo box. You're not even supposed to have one of those in school."
    Click. "Mumble mumble asshole mumble mumble."[13]

While the personal authority of teachers was diminishing as part of a larger cultural shift, it was being further curtailed by judicial decisions that conferred new rights on students. Public schools could no longer impose routine punishments like suspension without going through elaborate procedures and risking unpredictable liabilities. In some large school systems today, a pupil can assault a teacher without fear of reprisal, since the school does not dare to punish the pupil and the teacher knows that any use of force against a pupil, even in self-defense, is legally hazardous. Not surprisingly, assaults on teachers are not uncommon in those systems; there is a monthly form for reporting them.

    Besides the encouragement of active disorder, the decline of the teacher's authority has a milder but equally baneful effect on attitudes in the classroom. Here is a glimpse of an English class in a suburban high school, one of the best schools in a system nationally known for its quality.

There are more D's and F's than B's and C's on the grade sheets for English literature and few of the 17 high school juniors in room C112 mask their disgust. Cynthia Spink makes a show of ripping hers in half. Teacher Peggy Pfeiffer tries to be encouraging, "There is plenty of time for people to bring these up," she says before turning to a homework assignment few have done.

"I'm bored," says Christine Saffell. "I don't have my book, so it is not very thrilling for me."

A burly football player waltzes over to a table and retrieves a staple which he patiently pokes through his ear lobe. Three of his oblivious classmates have their heads on their desks.[14]

One of the most conspicuous of the changes in the outside world that has not been matched in the classroom was the phenomenal growth of information technology after 1970. Teaching machines were among the earliest developments in this technology but soon afterwards the improvement of microcomputers made the specialized teaching machine obsolete. All that is required today for machine-aided instruction and study is a microcomputer and some inexpensive software. The public schools have been slow to seize this opportunity to improve productivity. In 1990, U.S. high schools had one microcomputer for every 21 students. Only 39 percent of the students had ever used a computer in school; only 12 percent had used a computer for school work at home.[15]

The possibilities of videotape, compact discs, scanners and other electronic devices for instructional purposes are even more neglected. The videoscreen has not even begun to replace the blackboard and the chalk eraser in the American classroom. For students who have been bombarded with hi-tech audiovisual displays since infancy, the presentation of material in the schools is dull and primitive. Yet the system stubbornly clings to its archaic methods of delivering information.

There is little that the individual teacher can do about any of these large problems. Decisions about teaching methods and school organization are the prerogative of administrators above the level of the classroom teacher and the school principal. In large school systems, administrators are far removed from the day-to-day life of the classroom and concerned with such issues as school construction and closing, public relations, the politics of budgeting, racial incidents, salary policy, meeting federal and state mandates, insurance and litigation, union negotiations, and the like. Since the educational productivity of a public school system is not routinely measured, there is no incentive for administrators to be especially concerned with it. They are judged by their ability to increase their budgets and to minimize crises. Poor educational performance is not defined as a crisis. Meanwhile, the dead weight of excessive administration weighs heavily on teachers and principals.

Every year, the Virginia Department of Education sends the central office a forty-nine page book entitled *Calendar Reports*, which lists more than 300 reports that school headquarters has to make to Richmond during the year. Included are such items as "Application for Aid to Pay Instructional Costs for the School Community Cannery," "Emergency Immigrant Count," and "Report of Assaults on School Personnel."[16]

Successful schools depend heavily on parental involvement, if only because the parent-teacher coalition has better information and more power than either parent or teacher alone. The formation of that coalition depends on the individual teacher, not on remote bureaucracies. When teachers have some degree of professional autonomy, they have strong incentives to encourage parental involvement because it makes their work so much easier. But public school teachers have very little autonomy of any kind. They regard themselves as professionals and are so classified by the Bureau of the Census but they lack most of the attributes that identify a profession: an occupational monopoly enforced by practicing members of the profession, the help of trained assistants, high prestige, discretion about task priorities and work methods, and exemption from menial duties, among other things. The working conditions of public school teachers do not compare favorably with those of any skilled blue-collar occupation. Teachers are closely supervised, tightly scheduled and arbitrarily evaluated. Most of them have no paid helpers at all. They are routinely assigned to extra duties without extra pay. A formidable quantity of mindless clerical work is required of them. They have very little discretion about how to organize their own work. Their self-esteem is continuously threatened by unruly pupils, arbitrary supervisors, irrational rules, indignant parents and an unfavorable public image. Not an easy row to hoe.

The teacher occupies but a lowly place in the bureaucratic order. He or she reports to a department head, who reports to the assistant curriculum specialist in the central office, who reports to the curriculum specialist, who reports to the director of secondary education, who reports to the assistant superintendent for instructional programs, who reports to the superintendent. . . . When math teacher Mary Jackson wanted to reverse the order in which she taught two chapters from the standard math textbook, it was two months before the change was approved.[17]

The pay is not very good either. The average starting salary for teachers in 1992 was $22,171. It has more than kept up with inflation in the past 20 years but remains significantly below the starting salaries of college graduates who go into accounting, engineering, business administration or sales.[18] (However, the vacations are longer than in other occupations.) The terminal salaries in teaching are lower than in most other educated callings, and that is one reason why so many of the most promising new teachers leave within five years.[19]

These are the problems that beset teachers in the "good" public schools that provide elementary and secondary education in most American communities. But there are schools and entire school systems that have ceased to offer any meaningful service except daytime custody of their inmates. Consider the condition of the Chicago school system, sued in 1993 by a group of parents for failing to provide the high quality public education guaranteed by the Illinois constitution:

The average graduation rate in Chicago's public schools is 43.7 percent, 43 percentage points below the statewide average. Less than one of every three Chicago public high schools has a graduation rate above 50 percent. About 70 percent of public school students score below the national norms in standardized tests of basic skills, and substantially below statewide averages. Thirty-eight percent of the 64 high schools have ACT college admission test scores in the bottom one—yes, one—percent of the nation.

Chicago's bureaucratized system expends $5548 per pupil, about $750 more than the statewide average, but only 56 percent of the total budget goes for classroom instruction. The parents' brief notes that private schools provide better cognitive results at less per pupil expense "in the same neighborhoods as the city's worst public schools and draw from the same student population."[20]

The students in Chicago high schools are predominantly poor and predominantly black. The Chicago public school system, like most of those in America's largest cities, is a segregated system, with only a token representation of non-Hispanic whites. This is an ironic outcome of the long and valorous effort to desegregate the public schools that began with the *Brown* v. *Board of Education* decision in 1954 and culminated in the desegregation plans enforced by the federal courts in the 1970s. That effort was not futile. Throughout the United States, legal segregation was effectively prohibited. The majority of schools, public and private, were successfully integrated; that is, they accepted pupils without distinction of race or ethnicity, guaranteed them equal treatment and experienced very little ethnic conflict. But in the central cities of the largest metropolitan areas, school systems were resegregated by the operation of more or less natural causes.

Metropolitan areas everywhere are segregated by economic level because of steep gradients in land values and by ethnicity, because ethnic neighborhoods are large enough to develop a full set of institutions. This tendency is enhanced in American metropolitan areas by the administrative independence of suburban communities from the central city. Between 1930 and 1990, great numbers of blacks migrated to the central cities of the largest metropolitan areas. In the six largest American cities, the mean percentage of black residents increased from 9 percent in 1930 to 37 percent in 1990, while Hispanics increased from a negligible proportion in 1930 to 21 percent in 1990.[21] Thus, "minorities" are now the majority in these cities and in many others. Since blacks and Hispanics are more prolific than whites, they represent an even larger share of the youth population. But there is more to it than that. When white children in the public schools of the central cities became a minority, their parents fled to the suburbs, until almost none were left.[22] In the public schools of the same six cities in 1990, the average proportion of minority students in 1990 was a staggering 83 percent.[23] For Chicago, the figure was 88 percent. In the public schools of Washington, D.C., fewer than 1 percent of the pupils are white; the children of white government workers are to be found in the integrated schools of Arlington and Bethesda, along with the children of the affluent black and Hispanic families who joined the flight to the suburbs.[24] Today's segregated minority districts, unlike those of yesteryear, are occupied only by the poor, and it is they who enjoy nearly exclusive occupancy of the nation's worst schools.

Even outside the metropolitan cities, inequity is conspicuous in primary and secondary education since the public schools, largely supported by local property taxes, spend much more per pupil in rich districts than in poor districts, ingeniously giving the scantiest education to those who need it most.[25] The inequitable distribution of school expenditures makes the U.S. educational system less egalitarian than that of any other developed country. To the advantages that affluent students enjoy anyway because they have more social support, more comfortable settings and better equipment for out-of-school learning,[26] our system adds in-school advantages that make the gap between the children of prosperous, educated parents and the children of disadvantaged parents almost unbridgeable. And since the latter are disproportionately black and Hispanic, educational inequality translates directly into racial and ethnic inequality.

Any equalization of support between rich and poor districts is generally taken to imply an enormous increase in the total cost of the public school system since what is implicitly proposed is to bring the unfavored schools up to the level of the favored schools rather than to bring the favored schools down to a common average. Under existing conditions, the cost would indeed be stupendous but the point is that the existing conditions ought to be changed and productivity increased.

During the period when educational productivity stagnated, the cost of education never stopped increasing. The growth of school budgets puts continuous pressure on state and local budgets. That growth was explained by a steady decline in pupil-teacher ratios,[27] a steady increase in administrative burden, the rising cost of school construction, the imposition by federal and state mandate of new and costly programs such as bilingual instruction, and the fact that teachers' salaries outpaced inflation[28] without any improvement in productivity.

THE SEARCH FOR SOLUTIONS

In the 1980s, a long series of official and private reports lamented the parlous condition of teaching and learning in the public schools and proposed new incentives for teachers to teach and pupils to learn. The most influential of these tracts—one of four commission reports on educational reform that appeared in 1983 alone—was the report of the quasi-official National Commission on Excellence in Education, *A Nation at Risk*,[29] which cited the following "indicators of risk": in 19 separate cross-national tests, American students were never first or second compared to other developed countries, and were often last; many American adults and a sizeable percentage of American adolescents were "functionally illiterate"; the average achievement scores of high school students on standardized tests were lower than 20 years previously; the achievements of most gifted students did not match their tested ability; average scores on SAT College Board and science achievement tests had fallen steadily; many 17-year olds lacked "higher order" educational skills; and the demand for remedial courses had increased at all levels. The report lamented that secondary school curricula had been diluted and diffused to the detriment of useful instruction; only 31 percent of high school graduates completed intermediate algebra, only 6 percent took calculus. Their school time was wasted on trivial subjects such as "Training for Adulthood." The Commission found grade inflation everywhere, together with declines in graduation and college admission requirements, in the difficulty of subject matter, in the amount of homework assigned, in the intellectual level of textbooks and in the length of the school day. They criticized the way teachers were selected, trained and paid; discovered critical shortages in several fields; and claimed that half of all newly employed teachers in mathematics, science and English were unqualified.

The Commission proposed a reformed high school curriculum requiring all students to take four years of English, three years of mathematics, three years of science, three years of social studies, and a half year of computer science, and they specified the content of those "New Basic" courses. In less specific terms, they advocated more demanding instruction in elementary schools, better recruitment and training of teachers, more rigorous grading at all levels, more homework, longer school days and school years, more serious textbooks, more rigorous attendance policies, and stiffer college admission requirements. In somewhat veiled language, they advocated stricter classroom discipline, more tracking of students by academic ability and standardized nationwide tests. In their summing up, they wrote:

This Commission calls upon educators, parents and public officials at all levels to assist in bringing about the educational reform proposed in this report. We also call upon citizens to provide the financial support necessary to accomplish these purposes. Excellence costs. But in the long run mediocrity costs far more.[30]

The message was that an improved educational system would cost much more than the existing system, even though the existing system was absurdly expensive.[31]

The three other commission reports published in the same year made many other proposals for reforming elementary and secondary education, most of them along the same general lines: more work demanded of students, better-qualified people recruited to teach, more state and federal intervention, more money for all purposes.[32] The proposals that won the most political support were to reform teachers by awarding merit pay and master teacher status to the best of them and excluding the worst by tests of minimum competency. Within the teaching profession, the 1986 report of the Holmes Group, a committee of education school deans, attracted wide interest.[33] It proposed to enhance professionalization by requiring a bachelor's degree in liberal arts for entry into schools of education together with internships and certifying examinations for entry into the profession. Another group of critics advocated democratization—more of a voice for students, more autonomy for teachers, less emphasis on written regulations.[34]

This activity was not without results. In a 1988 survey of a large national sample of teachers,[35] solid majorities (59 percent or better) said that the clarity of goals, academic expectations for students and the leadership of the principal had improved in their schools during the previous five years; that student achievement in math, reading and writing was better; that core requirements for graduation had been raised, especially in science and math; that programs for disadvantaged *and* for gifted students were better; that textbooks and instructional materials had improved; that there was more achievement testing for promotion and graduation; and that their own salaries had been raised. After all this, 79 percent of the teachers in the survey gave the education reform movement a grade of C or worse.

That surprising outcome seems to be explained by the deterioration of working conditions caused by the reform effort. The teachers in the sample reported heavier teaching loads, more preparation time, larger classes, less time with colleagues, more nonteaching duties, more political interference, more state regulation, more bureaucratic paperwork, and less parental and community support.

A more reliable measure of the effects of the educational reform movement of the 1980s can be obtained from the National Assessment of Educational Progress, which administered the same proficiency tests in reading, mathematics and science to representative national samples of 9–year olds, 13–year olds and 17–year olds in the academic years 1979–80, 1983–84 and 1989–90.[36] For the population as a whole there were *no* significant changes during that decade, no improvement and no deterioration, although blacks and Hispanics showed minor gains in some subjects. Teaching is a highly routinized activity. Most teachers peaceably repeat the same lessons in the same way year after year while the debates about educational reform rage overhead.

The educational reform movement rolled on. In 1989, President Bush convoked the governors of all the states to an "Education Summit" at the University of Virginia. It was a brave sight. Out of that meeting came six National Education Goals for the year 2000 together with a profound sense of futility, since nobody imagined that the goals would be met. They were as follows:

— By the year 2000, all the children in America will start school ready to learn.

— By the year 2000, the high school graduation rate will increase to at least 90%.

— By the year 2000, American students will leave grades four, eight and twelve having demonstrated competence over challenging subject matter including English, mathematics, science, history, [and] geography, and every school in America will ensure that all students learn to use their minds well, so that they may be prepared for responsible citizenship, further learning, and productive employment in our modern economy.

— By the year 2000, American students will be first in the world in mathematics and science achievement.

— By the year 2000, every adult American will be literate and possess the knowledge and skills necessary to compete in a global economy and exercise the rights and responsibilities of citizenship.

— By the year 2000, every school in America will be free of drugs and violence and will offer a disciplined environment conducive to learning.[37]

Nothing in this program tells us how the perverse incentives for teachers not to teach too much and for students not to learn too much were to be overcome within a single decade.

As we marvel at these platitudes, let us remind ourselves how formidable the project of reforming the schools really is, and forgive the 50 governors for not developing a workable plan in three days. In the first place, there is no suitable agent to undertake the project on a national scale. American public schools are locally managed. Neither federal nor state governments are well positioned to reorganize a school. Their interventions are certain to increase administrative overhead but unlikely to change what teachers and pupils do in the classroom. Indeed, the whole concept of reform imposed from above is incongruous for a system in which problems are largely attributable to excessive administration. If significant changes are made, they will be made at the operating level, by teachers and pupils, parents and school boards, and the improvement of performance for the system as a whole will necessarily be slow and uneven.

In the second place, there is the virtual certainty of unintended and unwanted consequences when plausible reforms are introduced statewide or nationwide without careful testing. The two most popular reforms that came out of the 1983 commission reports, merit pay to reward outstandingly good teachers and competency testing to eliminate outstandingly bad teachers, illustrate this point. Merit pay, it appears, lowers the morale of teachers who are not so honored more than it raises the morale of those who are.[38] And since the unhonored are generally more numerous, the net effect of merit pay on teacher incentive is negative. Statewide competency testing is useless, rather than harmful. If passing scores were set high, the teaching force would be devastated and minority teachers would be hit especially hard. So, after a little fine-tuning, the passing score is set very low and the few teachers who fail are allowed to retake the test until they pass.

In the third place, the changes in the teacher-pupil relationship that are at the heart of the school crisis are rooted in social conditions over which the schools have no control and cannot acquire any control—the prevalence of television, the two-earner family, the growth of the urban underclass, the sexual revolution and the general decline of adult authority. No project of reform has any chance of success unless it takes account of these new conditions. There is no road back to 1960.

The limited competence of the public schools to build character, inspire good manners, encourage chastity or inculcate family values is a reflection of conditions in the larger society and nothing much can be done about it. But the teaching of reading, writing, arithmetic, science, history, languages, computer skills and other academic subjects can be improved almost without limit if attention is focussed on raising instructional productivity. The fundamental problems of the schools are not very different from those of other inefficient enterprises: archaic work methods, ineffective and bloated management, poor accounting and low accountability, output limitation by peer groups, and outmoded equipment. A private sector firm with these problems would either reorganize its operations or go out of business. In almost every such instance, successful reorganization turns out to require several interconnected actions:

— The accurate measurement of productivity

— The empowerment of the work force

— The modernization of equipment and work methods

— A leaner administration

In 1994 a few public schools in Minnesota and Massachusetts were turned over to private companies to run in the hope of achieving these purposes. Although the experiments are interesting, privatization is not likely to sweep the country. Successful reform, if it occurs, is more likely to come out of the existing educational system.

None of the measures I propose below are new. All of them have been introduced repeatedly in schools here and there and extensively discussed in the educational literature. But they have been tried one at a time and not conceived as the parts of a coherent plan for raising productivity.

The accurate measurement of productivity is the first and most essential step. The primary function of teachers is to improve the knowledge and skills of their pupils. As schools are presently organized, teachers have no way of evaluating their own performance of this primary function. An exceptionally bright pupil, or a dull one who is highly motivated, may give a teacher the illusion of success, but it is nearly impossible for that teacher, or anyone else, to compare the academic progress of a class during a school year with the progress of the class in the next room or with any other intelligible standard. How can people be expected to improve their productivity when they have no way of knowing what it is?

The single most important reform proposed for American schools is the establishment of national examinations, administered annually at all grade levels from kindergarten to twelfth grade and covering all the major subjects in the elementary and high school curriculum. It is also the easiest reform to accomplish. Such examinations have already been developed, not only in the foreign systems where they are routine, but in this country too. Assessment, as it is called in the educational literature, is used for all sorts of purposes— educational studies, tracking, admission to specialized schools— but it is not used to measure the achievement of individual pupils and classes against national standards or to measure the progress of individual pupils and classes from the beginning to the end of the school year. The national standards do not exist and the prospect of measuring academic progress class by class and year by year is alarming to principals and teachers. The few tests that have national norms—notably the SAT and ACT examinations—are designed for college admissions. Their coverage is limited to college applicants and they are not intended to measure annual progress. What they tell us about a national testing program is that it need not be, and probably should not be, a government program. A private organization can do the job as well, and with less political pressure. Moreover, there is room for more than one testing program, provided that each has sufficient coverage to establish national norms. Unlike the tests for college admissions, these national tests would be designed to measure academic improvement from point to point. They would be given at the beginning and the end of each school year and the scores reported for individuals and classes would be measures of relative improvement, expressed in percentile rankings, so that slow pupils could score better than gifted pupils if they had been effectively taught.

The absolute scores would be available also and they would give principals and teachers a much clearer picture of their instructional tasks than they can possibly obtain today. If pupils and their parents are to be actively involved in the effort to raise instructional productivity, then both sets of scores should be shown to them too. Although there are some risks in allowing disadvantaged students to discover the full measure of their disadvantage, a grading system that emphasized relative improvement would treat them a great deal better than they are treated now.

For pupils as well as teachers, the appropriate incentives must be sought within the school, not outside it. The dilemma is that the incentive to learn is easily stimulated in children and adolescents by turning the educational process into a contest, but eventually stifled in those contestants who never win. A shift from grading by achievement to grading by improvement would help. Given a fair contest, the great majority of children and adolescents are willing to play. But to be fair, the contest must award the prize it promises, which is enhanced competence.[39]

Standard tests of academic achievement and progress will automatically create a standard curriculum, roughly comparable to the national curricula that determine the content of schooling in countries with centralized educational systems. Wherever standard tests are adopted by a school or school system there will be much wailing and gnashing of teeth by teachers who are required to change their customary practices. One educational expert describes with entire approval how teachers in a magnet school resisted assessment of their teaching performance:

The development of a faculty culture helped teachers resist the imposition of standardized practices such as detailed curricular guidelines or district-wide final examinations (all of which ran counter to the purpose of the distinctive magnets).[40]

Another wrote that,

In its most ideologically offensive form, this type of prepackaged curriculum is rationalized as teacher-proof and is designed to be applied to any classroom regardless of the historical, cultural, and socioeconomic differences that characterize various schools and cultures.[41]

Despite resistance of this kind, the first halting step toward a national curriculum was taken in 1994 when Congress appropriated $100 million to establish national academic guidelines in all primary and secondary school subjects. The standards will be voluntary, but the money attached to them is sure to command the attention of school boards. Some form of nationwide achievement testing may eventually come out of this project.

The empowerment of the work force has a wider significance in a public school than in a factory. The usual reason for empowering a work force is to overcome output limitation by peer groups at the operating level. But output in schools is limited by peer groups at two operating levels—teachers and students. The experience of industry suggests that while output limitation can never be entirely eliminated, it can be held to a tolerable level by giving workers more voice in designing production methods and more autonomy in executing them. If this principle were applied to the public schools, groups of teachers would decide how to organize their collective task, individual teachers would decide how to achieve optimum progress with their students. But at the teachers' level, the problem of how to maintain order currently takes precedence over the problem of how to remove restrictions on output.

As we saw above, the personal authority of teachers over pupils has been greatly reduced by a combination of factors: the general decline of personal authority in the larger society, restriction of the penalties that a teacher can impose and the weakening of the parent-teacher coalition by changing family patterns. None of these trends can be reversed by anything done or left undone in the schools. But they leave teachers with insufficient power to get their jobs done. The obvious remedy is to send reinforcements into the classroom. Just as no self-respecting doctor would run his office without a nurse, no teacher should be expected to run a classroom without an aide. As every schoolboy knows, two adults are immeasurably stronger than one.

The example of the most successful foreign schools suggests that teachers are most effective when they prepare and give formal lessons to the entire class.[42] Such lessons have a beginning, a middle and an end. They cover a stated topic. They are not interrupted by band practice or tutoring. The same examples suggest that teachers should not try to give more than three or four class lessons in a day. The rest of their working time is needed for preparation and for consultation with colleagues.

Supervising a study hall or a cafeteria, working with individual students while the class sits idle, grading objective tests and filling out attendance reports are not appropriate professional tasks. They should be performed by aides. A school that now has one teacher for every 15 pupils could operate much more efficiently with one teacher and two aides for every 30 pupils.

The average classroom teacher in the United States earned $35,582 in 1992[43] for a work year that averaged 173 days of 7.3 hours in school. Their average pay per school hour was $28. (Their real hourly pay was lower, because of unpaid overtime and work taken home, but that is not relevant to the calculation here.) Under current conditions, as many well-qualified aides as are wanted can be hired anywhere in the United States at $10 an hour, either part-time or full-time. Replacing every two teachers in an average school by one teacher and two aides would increase the total adult presence by 50 percent and at the same time reduce the wage bill.

The requirements for appointment as an aide would be a degree from a two-year or four-year college, good character references and an interest in children. Some school systems, especially those with large minority populations, might want to do most of their recruitment among school parents, although aides would never be assigned to the same classrooms as their children. Aides might also be recruited from among college juniors and seniors, new education graduates, mothers of preschool children, retired workers of both sexes, and others who would like a rewarding and socially useful job. Aides would not be permitted to teach classes, even occasionally. That function would be restricted to professionally trained teachers. But aides could help individual students, introduce them to computer procedures, administer tests, supervise study halls and cafeterias, fill out reports and do all the other things that now distract teachers from their primary task.

In a school organized on this basis, the average class will be larger than it is now—almost as large as classes were 40 years ago when American public schools were the best in the world—but there will be two or three adults in the classroom and more effective authority.[44]

The experience of foreign systems suggests that just as teachers cannot usefully give more than three or four intensive class lessons in a day, pupils cannot profitably absorb more instruction than that.[45] And since American children and adolescents can no longer be compelled to do much homework at home, that necessary activity should be moved into the school. In place of six classes, a study period and a recess, a more reasonable daily schedule for pupils might consist of three classes, three study periods and three short recesses. The study periods would be supervised by aides and at least two aides would always be present, not so much to keep order as to assist pupils engaged in review, drill and self-testing on their computers.

The serious application of information technology in the public schools implies a computer on every student's desk, together with a large videoscreen in every classroom, and a local network in every school that provides text and graphics for formal lessons, review modules for daily study, programmed learning sequences for all the subjects that require repetitive drill and a self-testing program attached to every formal lesson. Machine-driven instruction is faster, more effective and much cheaper than personal instruction for subjects that are learned in part by repetitious drill: arithmetic, mathematics, foreign languages, grammar, geography and music appreciation. It is equally useful for teaching the informational content of the laboratory sciences, although laboratory experience must be added. For subjects in which questions can have more than one right answer, such as history, literature and social studies, personal instruction is essential, but machine-aided study, review and testing is generally effective. The keeping of classroom and school records can be computerized, too. For teachers to become more productive, their work must be made less laborious, and that can be accomplished in this industry, as in every other, by mechanization. Teachers and aides should put their efforts into explanation, guidance and encouragement, while the machines do the dog work.

The equipment looks costly when it first appears in the school budget but it is very much cheaper than the professional labor it replaces. Each hour of electronic instruction that replaces an hour of teaching labor saves about 80 percent of the previous cost. As to quality, there is every reason to expect that electronic instruction will be *more* effective than present methods, when controlled and supervised by teachers who have fewer chores and more time for teaching.[46]

Another item of new expense in tomorrow's well-organized school will be the rooms where teachers work when they are not in class. Every teacher has a private desk there. Every desk has a computer and a modem connection to a good library, and there are printers, scanners and copying machines close by. This is where lessons are prepared and reviewed, colleagues are consulted, references are checked, and problems are sorted out. In large high schools, every department will have its own teachers' room. In small elementary schools, there may be only one.

These simple innovations—national tests in all important subjects at the beginning and end of the school year, enhancing the authority of teachers by giving them continuous support in the classroom and relief from menial tasks, and the full use of information technology for instruction and study—are the essential steps to get the educational productivity of the public schools moving upward again. But there are some other useful things that could be done.

The experience of American industry in the recent past suggests that administrative bloat and bureaucratic rigidity can be cured by a drastic, high-handed reduction of administrative personnel. Some companies have arbitrarily reduced their headquarters staffs by 90 percent and become more profitable thereby. School administrators have tenure rights and cannot be laid off so casually, but a hiring freeze can accomplish the same purpose over a period of time. There is probably no large school system in the United States that would not run more smoothly if the size of its central administration were reduced by three-quarters and its administrative reporting was appropriately computerized. The money saved could be put to better use at the operating level.

The empowerment of students is not generally given as high a priority as the empowerment of teachers, if only because students in the public schools already seem to have too much power vis-à-vis teachers. But if the performance of teachers can be enhanced by allowing them more voice in the management of their own work, the same must certainly be true of students. In some foreign school systems, every class has a student leader who is responsible for discipline and who serves as spokesman for the class. In a curriculum oriented toward measurable achievement on national tests, there is considerable room for choice by students: for example, as to the order in which topics are studied, the amount of time given to review, the frequency of quizzes and the organization of study hours. Another way of empowering students is to enlist the most advanced students as tutors for their slower classmates or for students in lower grades. And heavy reliance on study groups is already the practice that identifies the best teachers in most of our schools.

The reader may have noticed the difficulty I have had in settling on a single term for the young people who are taught in the public schools. It seems inappropriate to refer to first-graders as students or to high school seniors as pupils. That difficulty reflects the wide cultural divide that separates elementary schools from high schools. The elementary school is a place where children are sent to acquire basic intellectual skills. The high school is a place where adolescents go more or less voluntarily for excitement, sociability, sexual opportunity, social climbing, personal display, intellectual excitement, athletic participation, training in the arts, practical information, political experience and vocational preparation, and to qualify for higher education. It is a microcosm of the larger community in which instruction must compete with many other activities that are more salient for students much of the time. To make any fundamental change in a high school is a herculean project. Moreover, most of the educational problems of high schools do not originate there. In nearly every American high school, there is a large group of students who never learned to listen to lessons or acquired the habit of study. In most high schools, there is a sizeable contingent of students who cannot read, write or calculate with any facility. At that stage in their lives, very few of them can be helped within the framework of the high school.

Reform efforts must concentrate on the elementary schools. Not only are they more amenable to improvement but every improvement at that level does more to solve the educational deficiencies of the middle schools and high schools than anything that can be done later on. Within the elementary school, it is in the first four grades that the need to improve instruction is most obvious. The children who have not learned to read or write easily by the time they reach the fifth grade cannot be brought up to a satisfactory level in any subsequent grade without a great deal of expensive special instruction that probably will not be available for them, whereas those who are able to read, write and calculate at the average level in the fifth grade are good prospects for satisfactory performance all the way through high school.

Whether still more can be achieved by starting formal instruction in nursery school and kindergarten remains an open question. The experience of Head Start, a program based on the assumed value of precocious study, has been mixed and rather inconclusive. There have been literally hundreds of studies of Head Start outcomes. Some show permanent benefits, some do not, but those that show benefits seem to agree that they are rather modest.[47] Some very successful foreign systems, like the Japanese, do not attempt any serious teaching before the first grade while other systems, like the French, require all children to attend preschools.

With or without earlier schooling, grades one through four are crucial. They are also better suited for innovation than the other levels of the K-12 sequence. The pupils are more manageable, the learning tasks more explicit and the equipment simpler. The most urgent task for the public schools is to use those four years to teach reading, writing and arithmetic so effectively that nobody is left behind.

NOTES

1. *Statistical Abstract of the United States, 1992* (hereafter *SAUS*), Tables 221, 222, 238, 245. There is also a public preschool sector that is

growing rapidly. About a million small children are enrolled in public nursery schools. Ibid., Table 236.

2. Office of Technology Assessment, 1989. Reported in *Washington Post* (December 3, 1989): C3.

3. One recent study indicates that U.S. parents rate low school achievement by their children more favorably than Japanese parents rate high achievement by theirs. Harold W. Stevenson and James W. Stigler, *The Learning Gap* (New York: Summit Books, 1992).

4. The percentages that represent the size of the private school sector have not changed appreciably since 1960. Per capita expenditure in U.S. private schools in 1990 was $3,329 compared to $4,955 in the public schools. *SAUS92*, Tables 211, 227.

5. For evidence on this point, see the comparison of attitudinal responses in public and private schools in National Center for Education Statistics, *Private Schools in the United States: A Statistical Profile, with Comparisons to Public Schools* (Washington, DC: U.S. Department of Education, 1991).

6. Based on U.S. Bureau of the Census, *Historical Statistics of the United States: Colonial Times to 1970*, Series II (Washington, DC: GPO, 1975), 598–661 and *SAUS88*, Table 232. These two official sources give slightly different figures; the latter shows a peak at 1970 instead of 1965, both show a slight decline after 1970.

7. Educational Resources Information Center (U.S.), *Mathematics Report Card: Are We Measuring Up?* (Princeton, NJ: Educational Testing Services, 1988).

8. National Center for Education Statistics, *The Condition of Education 1990*, Vol. 1; *Elementary and Secondary Education* (Washington, DC: U.S. Department of Education, 1991). The 1992 study was reported in Mary Jordan, "Students Test Below Average," *Washington Post* (February 6, 1992): A1, A4. The source was the Educational Testing Service.

9. U.S. Department of Education, *International Education Comparisons* (Washington, DC: Office of Policy and Planning, 1992).

10. Fervent testimony to this effect may be found in U.S. Congress, *Report of the Joint Economic Committee*, 100th Cong., 2d sess., 1988, Prt. 100–139.

11. Victor S. Vance and Phillip C. Schlechter, "The Distribution of Academic Ability in the Teaching Force: Policy Implications," *Phi Delta Kappan* (September 1982): 22–27.

12. Theodore Caplow "The Decline of Personal Authority in Four Industrial Societies," in *Convergence or Divergence*, edited by Simon Langlois (Frankfurt am Main: Campus Verlag, Montreal: McGill-Queens University Press, 1994).

13. James Nehring, *"Why Do We Gotta Do This Stuff, Mr. Nehring?" Notes from a Teacher's Day in School* (New York: M. Evans, 1989), 24.

14. Lisa Leff, "At Bethesda–Chevy Chase, Few Feel the Urge to Excel," *Washington Post* (April 5, 1992): A1, A22.

15. *SAUS92*, Tables 240, 241, 242.

16. Patrick Welsh, *Tales Out Of School* (New York: Viking), 179.

17. Ibid., 181.

18. *SAUS93*, Table 245.

19. For an illuminating discussion of teacher attrition, see Susan J. Rosenholtz, "Political Myths about Education Reform: Lessons from Research on Teaching," *Phi Delta Kappan* 66 (1985): 349–355. The recruitment problem is compounded, as it happens, by a retention problem. There is some evidence that the teachers with the poorest test scores are less likely to quit the profession. See, for example, Richard J. Murnane et al., *Who Will Teach? Policies that Matter* (Cambridge, MA: Harvard University Press, 1991), chapter 5.

20. George Will, "When the State Fails Its Citizens," *Washington Post* (March 7, 1993): C7.

21. The 1930 figures are from a special report by Charles E. Hall, *Negroes in the United States* (Washington, DC: U.S. Bureau of the Census, 1935); the 1990 figures are from *SAUS92*, Table 38.

22. William Frey, "Central City White Flight: Racial and Nonracial Causes," *American Sociological Review* 44, no. 3 (1979): 425–448.

23. Based on National Center for Education Statistics, *Digest of Education Statistics 1992*, NCES 92–097, Table 8.8. The six cities were New York, Los Angeles, Chicago, Houston, Philadelphia and Detroit, although in 1990, Detroit had fallen to seventh place, behind San Diego.

24. Kathryn P. Nelson, *Recent Suburbanization of Blacks: How Much, Who, and Where*, HUD PDR 378(2) (Washington, DC: Department of Housing and Urban Development, Office of Policy Development and Research, 1979); Thomas A. Clark, *Blacks in Suburbs* (New Brunswick, NJ: Center for Urban Policy Research, 1979).

25. The situation was brought to public attention by an eloquent best-selling book published in 1991. See Jonathan Kozol, *Savage Inequalities: Children in America's Schools* (New York: Crown, 1991).

26. Data from the 1989 Current Population Survey provide a spectacular example: fewer than 6 percent of high school students with household incomes under $20,000 use computers at home for school work, compared to 53 percent of students with household incomes over $75,000 (*SAUS91*, Table 247). The classic essay on the advantages of affluent students is Pierre Bourdieu and Jean-Claude Passeron, *The Inheritors: French Students and their Relation to Culture*, translated by Richard Nice (1964; Chicago: University of Chicago Press, 1979).

27. *SAUS93*, Table 239.

28. *SAUS93*, Table 245.

29. National Commission on Excellence in Education, *A Nation at Risk: The Imperative for Educational Reform* (Washington, DC: GPO, 1983). Three other commission reports on the same topic appeared in the very same year: Task Force on Education and Economic Growth, *Action for Excellence: A Comprehensive Plan to Improve Our Nation's Schools* (Denver: Education Commission of the States, 1983); The College Board, *Student Preparation for College: What Students Need to Know and be Able to Do* (New York: College Entrance Examination Board, 1983); and The Twentieth Century Fund Task Force on Federal Elementary and Secondary Education Policy, *Making the Grade* (New York: Twentieth Century Fund, 1983). For other accounts of the ills perceived and the cures proposed, see Roland S. Barth, *Improving Schools from Within: Teachers, Parents and Principals Can Make the Difference* (San Francisco: Jossey-Bass, 1990); Jeanne S. Chall, Vicki A. Jacobs and Luke E. Baldwin, *The Reading Crisis: Why Poor Children Fall Behind* (Cambridge, MA: Harvard University Press, 1990); Robert J. Marzano, C. L. Hutchins and U.S. Office of Educational Research and Improvement, *Thinking Skills: A Conceptual Framework* (Aurora, CO: Mid-continent Regional Educational Laboratory, 1985); Thomas Toch, *In the Name of Excellence: The Struggle to Reform the Nation's Schools, Why It's Failing, and What Should Be Done?* (New York: Oxford University Press, 1991); Lois Weis and others, *Crisis in Teaching: Perspectives on Current Reforms* (Albany, NY: State University of New York Press, 1989); Chester E. Finn, Jr., and Theodor Rebarber, eds., *Education Reform in the 90s* (New York: Macmillan, 1992).

30. Commission on Excellence in Education, *A Nation at Risk*.

31. In 1988, the United States spent more per pupil than any other developed country, except Switzerland, which spent approximately the same amount. Japan and West Germany, with conspicuously productive public school systems, spent only half as much per pupil as the United States. See U.S. Department of Education, *International Education Comparisons* (Washington, DC: Office of Policy and Planning, 1992), Table 3.

32. For a detailed comparison of the recommendations made by the four 1983 commission reports, see Lawrence C. Stedman and Marshall S. Smith, "Recent Reform Proposals for American Education," *Contemporary Education Review* 2, no. 2 (1983): 85–104.

33. The Holmes Group, *Tomorrow's Teachers* (East Lansing, MI: The Holmes Group, 1986).

34. Seymour B. Sarason, *The Predictable Failure of Educational Reform* (San Francisco: Jossey-Bass, 1990), Richard F. Elmore and Center for Policy Research in Education, *Restructuring Schools: The Next Generation of Educational Reform* (San Francisco: Jossey-Bass, 1990).

35. Carnegie Foundation for the Advancement of Teaching, *Report Card on School Reform: The Teachers Speak* (Princeton, NJ: Carnegie Foundation for the Advancement of Teaching, 1988).

36. *SAUS93*, Table 267.

37. Marzano, Hutchins and U.S. Office of Educational Research and Improvement, *Thinking Skills*.

38. Rosenholtz, "Political Myths."

39. The other solution, equally facilitated by national examinations, is to group students by level of achievement and let all of them compete at their own levels. That is essentially how our system of higher education is organized, and in that respect it works very well. But there are social and political objections to intensive tracking in the public schools.

40. Linda M. McNeil, "Exit, Voice, and Community: Magnet Teachers' Responses to Standardization," in *Crisis in Teaching: Perspectives on Current Reforms*, edited by Lois Weis et al. (Albany, NY: State University of New York Press, 1989), 161.

41. Henry A. Giroux and Peter McLaren, "Teacher Education and the Politics of Engagement: The Case for Democratic Schooling," *Harvard Educational Review* 56, no. 3 (1986): 219.

42. This point is admirably documented in the comparison of U.S. schools with their Japanese and Chinese counterparts by Stevenson and Stigler, *The Learning Gap*.

43. *SAUS93*, Table 238.

44. Although the reduction of class size has been the central policy of many American school systems for the past 20 years, and is strongly supported by teachers' organizations, the relationship between class size and student achievement is still exceedingly muddy. For an introduction to the vast debate on this matter, see Jennifer McGivern, David Gilman and Chris Tillitski, "A Meta-analysis of the Relation between Class Size and Achievement," *The Elementary School Journal* 90, no. 1 (1989): 47–56.

45. Ibid.

46. This assertion needs more supporting evidence than is presently available. It is remarkable that the Luddite resistance of teachers to machine-assisted instruction has so far inhibited any careful evaluation of it. I cannot find a single study that matches the results obtained by a competent teacher in any subject with the results of computer-assisted instruction in the same subject.

47. For an introduction to this vast literature, see R.H. McKey et al., *The Impact of Head Start on Children, Families and Communities* (Washington, DC: CSR Inc., 1985); Lawrence J. Schweinhart and David P. Weikart, "What Do We Know So Far?: A Review of the Head Start Synthesis Project," *Young Children* (January 1986): 49–55; Valerie E. Lee et al., "Are Head Start Effects Sustained? A Longitudinal Follow-up Comparison of

Disadvantaged Children Attending Head Start, No Preschool, and Other Preschool Programs," *Child Development* 61 (1990): 495–507.

5

WELFARE

WHAT IS WELFARE?

A broad view of the U.S. welfare system would have to include all of the federal and state programs whereby government agencies contribute to the incomes of selected categories of citizens: the pensions paid to retired workers and to handicapped people, public housing and rent subsidies, student aid and student loans, unemployment insurance payments, Medicare and Medicaid, guaranteed home mortgages, farm loans and subsidies, veterans' benefits, legal aid services, food stamps, and dozens of other government programs that provide income in cash or kind. The grand total of federal welfare expenditures for fiscal 1990 was $776 billion.[1] It is estimated that more than half of all U.S. households get income support of one kind or another from the government in any given year.

But most Americans do not think of Social Security or crop loans or student aid as welfare programs. They reserve the term for the joint federal-state program called Aid to Families with Dependent Children (AFDC), whose beneficiaries are persons under 18 and their mostly single mothers.

Contrary to popular belief, the cost of AFDC is only a tiny fraction of the grand total of welfare expenditures. It does not even loom very large among those programs intended to alleviate poverty.

The annual federal expenditure for family support payments, primarily in the form of AFDC, but also including child support collection programs, was budgeted at $11.2 billion in fiscal year 1990. This amount is only 9.0 percent of the poor welfare state and only 1.4 percent of the grand welfare state. Nonetheless, in the public mind and in political debate, AFDC receives most of the attention in discussions of "welfare"—indeed, it is almost a synonym for "welfare."[2]

The joint federal-state expenditure on AFDC in 1987, the latest year for which a full breakdown is available, was $16.3 billion, of which $2.1 billion went for administration, leaving $14.2 billion for distribution to the caseload of 11.1 million individuals, who received an average payment of $1,279 per year or $3,837 for a three-person family.[3] Contrary to another general impression, that benefit is much lower today than it was in the 1960s, and even with food stamps added, the average welfare family is much further below the poverty line than it used to be.[4]

There is a shocking difference between the amounts paid to welfare mothers to support their children and the amounts paid to middle-class foster parents when those same children are sent to live with them.

The current rate for foster-home care in the New York metropolitan area range from $386 to $526 per month for healthy children. For "special children" (those with moderate physical and/or mental disabilities) and "exceptional" children (those with illnesses like AIDS or other extreme physical or mental handicaps) the rates are $845 and $1,281 per month respectively. These stipends are tax free.[5]

AFDC payments vary from state to state; they are seven times as high in Alaska as in Alabama. Unlike Social Security and other federal entitlements, AFDC payments are not indexed to the cost of living and have not kept pace with inflation. Nearly all welfare families supplement their meager AFDC allowances with food stamps, fuel assistance, rent subsidies, help from relatives or unreported work. Many—not all—are enrolled with Medicaid. But there is no way for most of them to achieve a decent standard of living. Indeed, they are not expected to. Any display of material sufficiency, such as good clothes or new furniture, is likely to get them expelled from the program. In most states, recipients are not allowed to have more than $1,500 in disposable assets, thus assuring the perpetuation of their poverty. As Sherraden argues persuasively:

> If there is a culture of poverty, in my view, it is fundamentally asset-based. Slavery robbed blacks of the right to property and prevented their assimilation into the American culture of property ownership. Following slavery, institutions to facilitate and promote black wealth accumulation did not develop successfully. Indeed, to a large extent, social prejudices and banking institutions have systematically blocked asset accumulation among blacks.[6]

About 55 percent of AFDC recipients are black or Hispanic. About 55 percent have never been married. Very few are married now. About two-thirds live in households made up entirely of AFDC recipients; most of the rest share a household with relatives, most often a grandparent.[7] The people in the program are concentrated in large metropolitan areas. There were more than a million people on AFDC in California and about the same number in New York in 1987, but only a few thousand in Wyoming or New Hampshire.[8]

Fully half of AFDC mothers have two or more children and more than a third are taking care of a child under two. Very few are employed.[9] They have been on the rolls for a median of only 27 months but this figure obscures a sharp division among them. Short-term recipients, many of whom are recently divorced, use the program for a few months to tide them over until they find a husband or a job. For long-term recipients, most of whom have never been married, welfare is a way of life.

THE INCENTIVE STRUCTURE

Built into the laws and regulations that govern the welfare system are perverse incentives that make it impossible for the system to perform its ostensible function, which is to help poor parents to take good care of their children and eventually to escape from poverty.

Welfare recipients are powerfully motivated:

— Not to seek gainful employment
— Not to save
— If single, to remain single
— If married, to separate
— To cheat by concealing income and making other false reports

It is remarkable that so many of the women on welfare do eventually find husbands or jobs and leave the program, considering how the incentives are structured. The effective tax rate on the earnings of welfare recipients who sacrifice their eligibility to take a paying job is more than twice as high as the effective tax rate on an annual income of a million dollars. This chilling fact, first brought to public attention by Charles Murray (1984), was confirmed in painful detail in the 1991 report of the National Commission on Children (the Rockefeller Commission).[10]

The system is even more plainly misdesigned to discourage marriage. As the Rockefeller Commission showed, an unemployed woman on welfare who married her employed boyfriend with a $15,000 job would bring a financial calamity down on them both. Before they married, their combined net income after taxes was $18,598. If they married, their combined net income would be only $14,987.[11] The entitlements lost by the wife would be much greater than the small tax advantage gained by the husband.

Marriage to an AFDC recipient entails a heavy financial cost for an employed man and no economic benefit for his bride. Unmarried unions are even more costly for the woman. A woman on welfare who establishes a stable, unmarried union is likely to lose her welfare benefits without gaining any right to support from her partner.

The obvious lack of wisdom of these provisions has led to a good deal of legislative tinkering over the years, and under certain conditions a woman can now retain welfare eligibility while living with an unemployed husband or an employed boyfriend, but the conditions are too restrictive to make much difference.

Whether the welfare system, as presently organized, offers bounties for the production of children out of wedlock is a point that has been much debated. Welfare allowances are raised for each new child but the amounts are typically small and probably do not cover the additional cost. Nevertheless, several states are currently trying to reduce or eliminate additional payments for children born into families already on welfare[12] in the forlorn hope of preventing such births. A more convincing bounty effect occurs when an adolescent girl with a poor school record and no job prospects is enabled to set up her own household by having a baby and qualifying for welfare. There are many such cases but they do not account for a large share of the total caseload. Only about 1 in 30 welfare mothers is under 18; only 1 in 6 is under 21.[13]

The same source tells us that only 1 in 30 welfare mothers is over 45. AFDC payments end when the youngest child reaches 18. Only a handful of women over 45 remain on AFDC as guardians of grandchildren whose mothers have disappeared. A somewhat larger number make homes for daughters who receive welfare payments. Nobody knows what happens to the rest.

Another disputed question is whether the spectacular differences in AFDC allowances from one place to another induce potential welfare clients to migrate. States and cities paying higher benefits are said to be "welfare magnets" and to attract welfare clients from nearby places offering less favorable terms. For example, the high benefit levels of Wisconsin have apparently induced many Chicago residents to migrate to Kenosha and other places just over the Wisconsin state line.

The welfare magnet question has been extensively investigated. The early studies, conducted in the 1960s, showed that magnet effects were negligible. At that time, most states had residence requirements for welfare and newcomers could not obtain immediate benefits. After 1969, when the Supreme Court (in *Shapiro* v. *Thompson*) struck down all of the residence requirements, the situation apparently changed. Recent studies show strong and significant magnet effects.[14]

CAUSES AND CONSEQUENCES

Today's welfare system is the product of a long, unhappy evolution. Aid to Dependent Children (ADC) was introduced in 1935 as part of the original Social Security Act. It provided federal matching funds to the states to allow them to make cash payments for needy children. The intended beneficiaries were children left destitute by the death of their working fathers and the need was regarded as temporary.

The basic thinking of the social security reformers was that as OAI took hold, more and more elderly and widows would be covered and public assistance would wither. . . . By conceptualizing ADC as a problem to be solved eventually by the retirement program—white widows of working men would eventually be covered—the administration reflected both the thinking and the realities of that period. Divorced, deserted, and never-married women and women of color were simply not considered to be part of organized public welfare, rather, they and their children were lumped with the general mass of undifferentiated, undeserving poor.[15]

In the first 25 years, the program grew slowly and came to serve a population quite different than the children of poor white widows originally visualized. By 1960, the recipient population, which by then counted parents as well as dependent children (ADC became AFDC) had grown to only three million but in the decade that followed, the number almost tripled and the majority were unmarried black or Hispanic women and their children born out of wedlock. Under the joint impetus of the War on Poverty's "income policy" and an influential welfare rights movement, the rapid growth continued until 1975, when the recipient population peaked at 11.3 million. It has remained at about that level ever since.

By the end of the 1960s, the defects of the AFDC program were too conspicuous to ignore. From then until now, Congress and the state legislatures have continually tinkered with the rules in efforts to change the way the system induces poor women to stay single, avoid employment and bear more children. The most ambitious attempts to change the system were made by the first Nixon administration, which proposed a Family Assistance Plan that included a federally guaranteed minimum income for families with children and actually conducted field experiments with a prototype income maintenance program. Its effects on work effort and family solidarity turned out to be unfavorable.

The most important practical change of the 1970s was the addition of fringe benefits to the basic AFDC allowance: food stamps, the WIC (Women, Infants and Children) benefits, Medicaid, fuel assistance and rent subsidies. Welfare recipients now receive an individualized package of entitlements from multiple programs, each operated under different rules.

There were repeated attempts to reduce the incentives to remain single and to avoid employment that were built into the system. A small number of two-parent families with disabled or unemployed fathers were made eligible for AFDC under stringent conditions. Welfare mothers were allowed to earn a bit of money (typically $30 a month) without reducing their allowances. But these adjustments were trivial.

The basic dilemma remained. If AFDC clients were not adequately supported, their children would suffer. If they were adequately supported, their numbers would increase.

The substitution of workfare for welfare was loudly proclaimed in the 1980s. Program changes during the Reagan years were designed to lure or drive welfare mothers into the labor force, while collecting more support money from the absent fathers of their children. Neither idea was new.[16]

A Work Incentive Program (WIN) was enacted by Congress in 1967 to furnish job training and job search help to welfare clients. Mothers without preschool children and able-bodied males on AFDC (an almost imaginary category) were required to enter the program or lose their benefits. In practice, registration for WIN became one more meaningless formality in the mills of welfare administration. A more serious effort to introduce workfare was a 1981 act of Congress that allowed states to set up mandatory Community Work Experience Programs, elegantly known as CWEPs. Adults on welfare were required under these programs to participate in job training and "work experience activities" or lose their benefits. Additional legislation along the same lines was added in 1984 and 1987. Some of the job training programs were elaborate; more of them were perfunctory. None of them had much practical effect, since the jobs open to their graduates generally provided less income than the welfare package.[17] The tired workfare idea was the centerpiece of the Clinton administration's 1994 proposals for welfare reform, coupled with a two-year limit on benefits and a promise of public employment for women dismissed from the welfare rolls if jobs could not be found for them in the private sector. Such employment would almost certainly take on the same ritualistic character as the existing job training programs, but at much greater cost. Meanwhile, the federal government has granted Wisconsin a waiver to experiment in 1995 with a program that would limit single mothers to a single year of benefits and then let them sink or swim.

The effort to make absent fathers contribute to the support of their children on welfare also has a long history. Beginning in 1950, various pieces of federal legislation authorized or mandated states to pursue absent fathers and attempt to collect child support payments from them. The effort became more serious with a 1984 federal statute that required every state to take over the responsibility of obtaining support orders from state courts, to set guidelines for the courts to use in determining the amount of fathers' obligations, and to provide for the collection of delinquent support payments by garnishing wages, tax refunds, unemployment compensation and other income and attaching real and personal property. New federal agencies were established to oversee the new state agencies charged with these duties. This machinery was made available to all the custodial parents (i.e., mothers) of children with absent parents (i.e., fathers), not just to the AFDC population. As might be expected, it did much more for poor working mothers than for mothers on welfare, partly because the former were more likely to know the location of the absent father and he was more likely to be economically competent, partly because the AFDC mothers had little incentive to cooperate. Only the first $50 of monthly support payments collected on behalf of children on AFDC is passed through to the mother. The remainder is kept by the federal and state agencies to offset the cost of welfare payments. In other words, it is taxed at 100 percent. Families not on welfare get all of the child support payments made on their behalf, unless they have previously been on welfare, in which case some part of the support is used to reimburse the public agencies.[18]

The grand total of child support payments passed through to AFDC families nationwide in 1987 (the latest year for which there are published figures) was $251 million—about $22 per AFDC recipient.[19] In a number of states, the cost of administering the program exceeded the amount collected.[20]

In the early 1990s, as state budgets came under increasing pressure, at least a dozen states attempted to reform welfare by punitive measures: reducing allowances for children who were reported as truants; eliminating payments for additional children; reducing benefits for recipients who avoid job training, health checkups or other mandated behavior; or simply reducing benefits across the board.

The dilemmas of welfare policy are grounded on some remarkable demographic trends. From 1970 to 1992, the proportion of U.S. white adults reporting themselves as married declined from 73 percent to 64 percent and the proportion of married black adults from 64 percent to 43 percent.[21] Births to unmarried women increased from 399,000 in 1970 to 1,165,000 in 1990.[22] The percentage of all births that were illegitimate increased at a greater rate for whites (from 6 percent in 1970 to 20 percent in 1990) than for blacks, but the figure for blacks, starting much higher (38 percent in 1960), rose to the unprecedented level of 65 percent in 1990.[23]

Divorce, the other main source of families headed by young women, also increased somewhat during this period. Women almost invariably experience a sharp loss of income after divorce and are not likely to make it up unless they remarry.[24]

The result was a great increase in female-headed families. By 1992, there were 7 million female-headed white families with children under 18, 2.3 million black, about 800,000 Hispanic.[25] Most of them were dreadfully poor but the blacks and Hispanics were poorer. The average monthly AFDC caseload in 1989 was about 3.9 million: 40 percent white, 41 percent black, 15 percent Hispanic, and 5 percent "other."[26]

After allowing for the small number of two-parent families on AFDC, these percentages yield about 1.40 million white families on AFDC at any given time, or one-third of all white female-headed families with children. But the 1.43 million black families and 525,000 Hispanic families on AFDC are about two-thirds of the female-headed families in their respective groups.

Given the fairly high rate of turnover on the AFDC rolls, it is plain that at least half of the female-headed white families and nearly all female-headed black and Hispanic families with children under 18 are supported, at least intermittently, by AFDC.

The number of children born out of wedlock is not an exact indicator of the rate at which female-headed families are added to the population. Many such children acquire fathers or stepfathers soon after birth, or in the case of consensual unions, have an unmarried father already present when they are born. Many children born to married couples lose their fathers early in life by divorce, separation or death. These opposite effects tend to cancel each other out, so that there is a rough correspondence between births out of wedlock and the establishment of female-headed families. The increase in births to unmarried women from 1960 to 1990 was 449 percent.[27] The increase in female-headed households over approximately the same period was 242 percent, which is a fair match considering that the average single mother has about 2.2 children[28] and the average number of children in AFDC families is about the same.[29]

The situation is grave enough when only the white population is considered. A great many of the children of female-headed white families live in poverty. It is worse for the Hispanic population[30] and catastrophic for the black population, where nearly every female-headed family is poor. By 1991, 17 percent of all white children under 18, 27 percent of Hispanic children and 54 percent of black children lived in such families.[31]

There is no mystery about the poverty of female-headed families. Not only do women earn less than men but most unmarried mothers did not graduate from high school and have no marketable skills, while those on AFDC are forbidden to save.

Take the case of Grace Capitello, a 36–year old single mother with a true talent for parsimony. To save on clothing, Ms. Capitello dresses herself plainly in thrift store finds. To cut her grocery bill, she stocks up on 67–cent boxes of saltines and 39–cent cans of chicken soup. . . .

Ms. Capitello's stingy strategies helped her build a savings account of more than $3,000 in the last four years. Her goal was to put away enough money to buy a new washing machine and maybe one day send Michelle to college. . . . But there was one catch. Ms. Capitello is on welfare—$440 a month, plus $60 in food stamps—and saving that much money on public aid is against the law. . . . Last month, the Milwaukee Department of Social Services took her to court, charged her with fraud and demanded that she return the savings.[32]

On every conceivable measure of social adjustment or achievement, children brought up by a single parent do worse than those brought up by two parents. They are less likely to graduate from high school or go on to college, more likely to acquire a criminal record, more likely to become drug abusers, more likely to die by violence. Many of the boys will father children they will not support. Many of the girls will bear children out of wedlock. The single mother, however well intentioned, seldom has the material or psychological resources to raise a child as well as two parents can.

These negative outcomes are much the same for white AFDC children as for black and Hispanic children but the latter suffer additional disadvantages because of their concentration in urban "ghettos" and a degree of cultural isolation from the larger society. While white welfare recipients are thinly scattered across the land, black and Hispanic recipients are clustered in metropolitan cities, where their disproportionate numbers impose a heavy burden on public services and encourage the continued flight of upper- and middle-income families, both white and black, to the suburbs. More than 40 percent of all the pupils in the public schools of New York, Chicago, Philadelphia, Detroit and other large metropolitan areas are black children on AFDC.[33]

Additionally, the urban underclass is the object of unremitting hostility from low- and middle-income whites who see themselves as heavily taxed for the support of people who refuse to support themselves and who, in their view, have no moral claim to public support. The Edsalls (1991) maintain that this antipathy was a pivotal factor in the election of three Republican presidents in the 1970s and 1980s.

The severity of poverty for blacks in the bottom quintile has contributed to the growing perception that to be poor is to be black, a perception that offsets black gains in the middle class and which functions to confirm racial stereotypes held by whites. The conservative assault on means-tested programs and affirmative action has capitalized on white stereo-types about black poverty, and on white resentment of perceived black dependence on welfare and racial preferences.[34]

At the heart of the welfare reform problem is a moral and political dilemma defined by the concept of fairness and the arith-metic of wage distribution.[35] It does not seem fair that poor people who don't work at all should be paid as much as poor people who work full-time. Nor does it seem fair that little children should go hungry through no fault of their own. But since poor people who work full-time are barely able to keep their children fed (a single mother employed full-time at the minimum wage falls about 30 percent below the poverty line) welfare recipients who are given a decent level of subsistence must necessarily receive about the same incomes as their working neighbors.

Obviously, the typical welfare recipient cannot improve her life situation by moving from the welfare rolls to a low-paying job and, with meager education and little or no work experience, she is not going to find a high-paying job.

Although the ancient distinction between the deserving and undeserving poor is dismissed as a piece of archaic cruelty in current writings about poverty, it resurfaces in some form in nearly every discussion of welfare policy. The deserving poor are those who cannot be held responsible for their own poverty because they are unable to work for a living and cannot be held responsible for the condition that disqualifies them. They are too young or too old to work, or physically or mentally incapacitated, or involuntarily unemployed. Providing them with support from public funds does not activate the fairness dilemma. Historically, the undeserving poor were the "sturdy beggars" of the English Poor Laws, able-bodied males without legitimate occupation and the women who consorted with them. The widows of working men were presumptively deserving, especially if they had young children. As we have seen, that view still prevailed in the United States in 1935 when the Social Security Act was passed. As recently as then, welfare legislation took no cognizance of the unmarried women who were raising children by themselves. Unmarried adolescents who became pregnant were expected to give their babies up for adoption. Older women who bore children out of wedlock were presumed to be living in consensual unions. The population of single mothers was relatively small in the early days of ADC. There were only 90,000 live births to unmarried American women in 1940 compared with more than a million in 1990.[36] Some of those 90,000 babies were presumably raised in households with no other adult than their mother but they were few enough to be disregarded.

As the number of infants born to unmarried women steadily increased over the next 30 years and fewer of them had a father in the household,[37] the population of such families became too large to ignore. Most of them were poor, of course.[38] The children were deserving by definition. Their mothers were undeserving by definition, being themselves responsible for the condition that prevented them from working. But there was no way to support the deserving children without also supporting their undeserving mothers. The traditional "indoor relief" for infants born out of wedlock, the orphanage, was no longer acceptable, since it was now taken for granted that children would be better off living with their mothers than in an institution. The stage was set for the husbands to disappear from the homes of millions of poor women and for the government to take their place. The government was a rude and ungracious husband but much more reliable than a man with a low-paying, insecure job.

So long as this bizarre arrangement—the marriage of poor women to the government—is encouraged by official policy, the moral and political dilemmas of the welfare system cannot possibly be resolved. The only solution is to remove the government-sponsored incentives for unmarried women to bear children without any commitment from the children's fathers and the incentives for married men to abandon their wives and children.

These incentives would be even stronger, of course, without legal abortion. Five out of six abortions in 1988, the most recent year for which full data are available, involved unmarried women. If all of those pregnancies had gone to term, the number of births to unmarried women would have risen from 1 million to 2.32 million.[39] Without abortion, there would have been perhaps twice as many AFDC recipients.

THE SEARCH FOR SOLUTIONS

The only way out of the trap that well-intentioned legislators have constructed for young women and for society itself is to change the incentive structure so that it becomes less disadvantageous for poor people to marry and to raise their children together.

This will not restore the low illegitimacy rates of 1940. The social controls on childbearing have been too far relaxed. Today's norms give men and women an absolute right to reproduce that does not depend on any commitment from them to the unborn child. The draconian measures that used to discourage and penalize child-bearing out of wedlock are not likely to be restored. But something can be done about the worst defects of the existing system—its exorbitant tax rates and its ridiculous rules.

It is impossible to design a means-tested welfare program that does not encourage fraud, since recipients who report their earnings and expenditures honestly will get less money than those who misreport. It is equally impossible—within the existing wage structure—to design a means-tested program that is fair to nonrecipients, some of whom will get less for working full-time than recipients get without working at all. And it is arithmetically impossible to design a means-tested program that provides a decent standard of living for female-headed families and does not discourage marriage. Here is a participant's understanding of how these dilemmas converge:

You asked me what I thought of welfare, if I had ever thought of going on welfare. Well, I actually applied for food stamps and AFDC after the accident. But because I am living with my grandmother and not paying rent, they said they could only give me food stamps. But if I moved into my own place, I'd really be worse off even with AFDC. . . . Besides when they found out that my grandmother had assets and property, I was told that as long as I lived with her I couldn't qualify for even food stamps because she could always liquidate her assets. I can't ask her to do that. . . . It's just weird, it's like a Catch-22. If I went out and got an apartment, they would give me AFDC and food stamps, but there really wouldn't be enough to pay my rent and everything else. If I worked, then I wouldn't be eligible for anything. Yet, even working, I wouldn't have enough to pay a babysitter and everything else without some kind of help, like food stamps.[40]

Other modernized countries do not face these intractable problems because they provide financial support for all children without regard to their parents' incomes. Levitan summarizes the situation thus:

Other advanced industrial nations annually spend roughly 1 to 3 percent of their gross domestic product on cash family benefits; this is equivalent in the United States to about $50 billion to $150 billion. . . . Although comparative data on family allowances among the major industrial democracies are subject to numerous arbitrary adjustments, they indicate that the United States lags far behind other advanced countries.[41]

Under a family allowance system, poor men are motivated to marry because marriage enhances their incomes. Single mothers are motivated to work for the same straightforward reason. Administrative costs are negligible and fraud is almost unknown. In Germany, where the government pays a substantial allowance for every child in the country, the illegitimacy rate is about a third[42] of the American rate and the overwhelming majority of children live with both parents. The total cost for 1989 was about $90 billion.[43] That system is by no means trouble-free and has recently been subject to retrenchment[44] but its problems are trivial compared to those of the U.S. system.

There are 64 million persons under 18 in the United States; about 40 percent of them are first children. Suppose that every employed custodial parent and every married couple received a wage or salary supplement of $3,000 for their first child and $2,000 for each later child, paid by the federal government and uniform throughout the country.[45] The allowance could decline by 10 percent for each $5,000 of taxable income, phasing out entirely at a taxable income of $50,000. This would cost the Treasury about $80 billion annually but that outlay would be partly offset by savings in AFDC payments, food stamps and other welfare benefits; by a great reduction in administrative costs; by the abolition of the existing deduction for dependent children; and by the additional taxes paid by middle- and upper-income recipients on their family allowances. The net cost after these offsets should not exceed $30 billion, a serious but manageable burden, with the promise of many eventual savings.

There are some agreeable features of this plan that do not appear at first glance. Gone would be the rigmarole of eligibility rules and the micromanaging of other people's budgets by social workers. The amount of each year's allowance would be based on last year's pay stubs or tax returns. The marginal tax rate on additional earnings would be too low to discourage anybody from working. The restrictions on the accumulations of assets would be lifted; saving and home ownership would be actively encouraged. The welfare magnet effect would be reversed, since family allowances would go a lot further in low-rent areas away from the big cities.

A more generous system of family allowances, on the German model, is out of our present reach, for several reasons. First, it would cost more than the straitened federal budget could sustain. Second, fairness requires that the family allowance of a nonworking mother not exceed the take-home pay of a man or woman working full-time at or near the minimum wage. Third, the level proposed would give most AFDC mothers about as much income as they now receive from AFDC and food stamps together. It would not lift them out of poverty but they would have a real opportunity to do it themselves, since there would no longer be a financial penalty for taking a job or taking up with a man.

The family allowances would be disregarded in determining eligibility for Medicaid, if universal health insurance had not become available in the meantime. Medicaid covers only a fraction of its eligible clients, and often treats them badly, but it would make no sense to deprive female-headed families of that protection.

The details of a family allowance system are less important than the underlying principle.[46] The effort to support very poor children without offering any support to children who are nearly as poor has led directly to the overproduction of very poor children and the creation of millions of very poor families. So long as the government pays good money for proof of poverty and takes the money away as soon as poverty begins to be overcome, poverty will be perpetuated and the nation will suffer for it.

This analysis may seem to vault lightly over many grave issues: the question of social justice, the structure of an economy in which low-paying service jobs have largely replaced high-paying factory jobs, the lack of vocational opportunities for people with less than a high school education, the defective performance of inner-city schools, the consequences of adolescent sexuality, the selective operations of the criminal justice system, the implications of moral tutelage by social agencies, the importance of welfare as a political icon, and the racial hostility barely concealed in most measures of welfare reform.

These issues are important and worthy of debate. But they do not offer solutions to the perennial welfare crisis. The existing welfare machinery is unworkable not only because it embodies competing social values but also because it rests on the false assumption that the poor do not make rational economic choices. Assume that they will and the problem becomes manageable.

NOTES

1. Michael Sherraden, *Assets and the Poor: A New American Welfare Policy* (Armonk, NY: M. E. Sharpe, 1991).

2. Ibid., 63.

3. U.S. Congress, Senate, Committee on Finance, *Data and Materials Related to Welfare Programs for Families with Children* (Washington, DC: GPO, 1988), 6 and Tables A-8, A-10.

4. Barbara Gottschalk and Peter Gottschalk, "The Reagan Retrenchment in Historical Context," in *Remaking the Welfare State: Retrenchment and Social Policy in America and Europe*, edited by Michael K. Brown (Philadelphia: Temple University Press, 1988).

5. Susan Sheehan, "A Lost Childhood," *The New Yorker* (January 11, 1993): 73.

6. Sherraden, *Assets and the Poor*, 138.

7. Older AFDC mothers tend to live alone with their children; younger mothers with small children often continue to live with their own mothers. U.S. General Accounting Office, *Relationships and Incomes in Households with AFDC Recipients and Others*, GAO/HRD-88-78 (1988).

8. Senate Committee on Finance, *Data and Materials*, Table A-8.

9. Ibid., Tables A-13, A-16.

10. National Commission on Children, *Beyond Rhetoric: A New American Agenda for Children and Families* (Washington, DC: National Commission on Children, 1991).

11. Ibid., Tables 5–1, 91.

12. The movement to deny additional benefits for women who give birth while on AFDC began in New Jersey in 1992.

13. Senate Committee on Finance, *Data and Materials*, S. Prt. 100–101, Table A-21. The figures are for 1985.

14. For an excellent summary of the welfare magnet studies, see Paul E. Peterson and Mark S. Rom, *Welfare Magnets: A New Case for a National Standard* (Washington, DC: The Brookings Institution, 1990).

15. Joel F. Handler and Yeheskel Hasenfeld, *The Moral Construction of Poverty: Welfare Reform in America* (Newbury Park, CA: Sage, 1991), 103–104.

16. For a detailed history of the long, futile effort to replace welfare with "workfare," see Andrew J. Polsky, *The Rise of the Therapeutic State* (Princeton, NJ: Princeton University Press, 1990), chapter 8.

17. Michael Wiseman, "Workfare and Welfare Reform," in *Beyond Welfare: New Approaches to the Problem of Poverty in America*, edited by Harrell R. Rodgers, Jr. (Armonk, NY: M. E. Sharpe, 1988).

18. Senate Committee on Finance, *Data and Materials*.

19. Ibid., Table 8–1.

20. The proportion of illegitimate births in which paternity is established at the initiative of the new public agencies varies enormously, from around 50 percent in the most energetic states to around 2 percent in the most indifferent. See James S. Denton, "Child Support Enforcement and Welfare Reform," in *Welfare Reform: Consensus or Conflict?*, edited by James S. Denton (New York: University Press of America, 1988).

21. *Statistical Abstract of the United States 1993* (hereafter *SAUS*), Table 59.

22. *SAUS93*, Table 101.

23. Ibid.

24. James P. Smith, "Poverty and the Family," in *Divided Opportunities: Minorities, Poverty and Social Policy*, edited by Gary D. Sandefur and Marta Tienda (New York: Plenum Press, 1988).

25. *SAUS93*, Tables 49, 53.

26. Daniel Patrick Moynihan, "Foreword," in Denton, *Welfare Reform*. Moynihan's figures for racial composition are for 1986, the caseload figure is for 1987 (from Senate Committee on Finance, *Data and Materials*, Table 4–7).

27. *SAUS79*, Table 58, and *SAUS91*, Table 58.

28. Based on *SAUS93*, Table 70.

29. Senate Committee on Finance, *Data and Materials*, Table A-16.

30. Hispanics are not a homogeneous population. The proportion of Puerto Rican families in the United States that are female-headed is about the same as for blacks; the proportion for Mexican Americans is much closer to that of whites. Theodore Caplow, *American Social Trends* (San Diego: Harcourt Brace Jovanovich, 1991), 191–192.

31. *SAUS92*, Table 69.

32. Robert L. Rose, "For Welfare Parents, Scrimping is Legal, but Saving is Out," *Wall Street Journal* (February 6, 1990): A1, A10.

33. Moynihan, "Foreword," xi.

34. Thomas Byrne Edsall with Mary D. Edsall, *Chain Reaction: The Impact of Race, Rights and Taxes on American Politics* (New York: W. W. Norton, 1991), 232.

35. A number of other value dilemmas are raised by the welfare system: outdoor versus indoor (institutional) relief, lumping versus categorizing, the attribution of blame to society or the individual, the conflict of punitive and compassionate impulses, and the unequal conditions in primary and secondary labor markets. See John L. Tropman, *American*

Values and Social Welfare: Cultural Contradictions in the Welfare State (Engle-wood Cliffs, NJ: Prentice-Hall, 1989), chapter 5.

36. U.S. Bureau of the Census, *Historical Statistics of the United States: Colonial Times to 1970*, Part I, Series B28–35 (Washington, DC: GPO, 1975); *SAUS91*, Table 92.

37. *SAUS93*, Table 113.

38. And limited in other ways, too. Fifty-nine percent of a national sample of unwed mothers scored in the lowest quintile of educational qualification in a 1985 study.

39. *SAUS93*, Table 737.

40. Leslie W. Dunbar, *The Common Interest: How Our Social Welfare Policies Don't Work and What We Can Do About Them* (New York: Pantheon, 1988), 118–119.

41. Sar A. Levitan, *Programs in Aid of the Poor*, 6th ed. (Baltimore: Johns Hopkins University Press, 1990), 73–74. Despite these comments, Levitan is not very enthusiastic about family allowances, for which he says, there is no constituency in the United States.

42. A rate of 9.7 percent in 1989.

43. Wolfgang Glatzer, Karl-Otto Hondrich, Heinz Herbert Noll, Karin Stiehr and Barbara Worndl, *Recent Social Trends in West Germany 1960–1990* (Frankfurt am Main: Campus Verlag, Montreal: McGill-Queens University Press, 1992).

44. Andrei S. Markovits and Jost Halfmann, "The Unraveling of West German Social Democracy," in Brown, *Remaking the Welfare State*.

45. The National Commission on Children (Rockefeller Commission) recognized the desirability of family allowances in its 1991 report but its recommended allowance (a $1,000 refundable tax credit for all children through age 18) would be too small to have much effect on the welfare population. See National Commission on Children, *Beyond Rhetoric*.

46. Except that the allowance cannot be so low as to defeat the intention of the program, like the $1,000 per child payments proposed by the Rockefeller Commission.

6

CRIMINAL JUSTICE

CAUSES AND CONSEQUENCES

The root cause of the perverse incentives that now dominate the criminal justice system of the United States is the attempt to prohibit the importation, sale and use of certain euphoriant substances. This is called the war on drugs. It has been greatly intensified in recent years, without any perceptible reduction in the availability of the forbidden merchandise. It has generated a truly remarkable set of perverse incentives.

The war on drugs has been unsuccessful in suppressing the demand for marijuana, heroin, cocaine, hallucinogens, amphetamines and related products, and equally unsuccessful in blocking the importation of these substances from the countries where they are produced—marijuana grown in Mexico, cocaine from coca leaves grown in Peru and Bolivia and processed in Colombia, heroin from poppies grown in Turkey and processed in France, among many other sources. But it does impose heavy risks on suppliers at all levels. Since they operate outside the law, they are unprotected against predation and fraud. Their goods are subject to confiscation or destruction at every stage from the grower to the ultimate consumer. They are open to extortion by informers and by corrupt enforcement agents and of course there is the constant risk of capture and imprisonment.

These extraordinary hazards warrant extraordinary compensation, and everyone involved in the trade from the grower to the street peddler expects and gets a much higher margin of profit than he could ever obtain by selling legitimate commodities. (According to the Drug Enforcement Agency, the cost of raw coca amounts to about 1 percent of the retail price of refined cocaine in the United States.) And since earnings from drug trafficking cannot be reported, they go untaxed. The vast sums generated in the wholesale end of the business enable major importers to arrange protection against the rigors of the law. Very few of them are arrested or prosecuted.

Retail dealers and small wholesalers also enjoy much higher earnings than they could expect to obtain in any legal line of work, and they can afford conspicuous luxuries, but they are not very well insulated from risk. Many, if not most, of them are eventually arrested and convicted, and serve time. They account for most of the recent spectacular rise in the U.S. prison population.

In 1960, the prison population was only 188,000, the lowest proportion of the general population in 40 years. It did not change appreciably until 1974; then it began to climb. There were more than 300,000 inmates in state and federal prisons by 1981, more than 400,000 by 1982, more than 500,000 by 1985, more than 600,000 by 1989. The number passed 800,000 in 1991, and there is no sign of a letup. Another 400,000 people were in jail in 1991, and that number is also increasing faster than new jails can be built. More than 2.5 million people are on probation and another half million on parole.[1] Staggering numbers.

The number of persons sentenced to state prisons for drug trafficking and possession rose by 559 percent in the seven years from 1982 to 1989, while the ratios of drug prosecutions to arrests and of prison sentences to prosecutions, as well as the length of sentences, increased sharply during the same interval.[2] The percent of all defendants sentenced to federal prisons who were convicted of drug trafficking passed 50 percent in 1990[3] and is still rising. The proportion of state defendants is a little lower but rising as fast.

Federal expenditures for the war on drugs increased from about $200 million in 1980 to more than $12 billion in 1992. Some of it went in subsidies to Bolivian peasants who were paid $2,000 a hectare to destroy their coca plantations. The simple-minded peasants pocketed the money and started new plantations down the road, so that their exports of coca increased.[4]

As the futility of the war on drugs became apparent and its frenzy heightened, the treatment of drug offenders became more punitive. Persons arrested for drug offenses are much more likely to be prosecuted, convicted and incarcerated than those arrested for violent crimes. Their sentences are often as harsh as those for rape and robbery, sometimes much harsher. In June 1991, the U.S. Supreme Court sustained the sentence of Ronald Harmelin, a first offender sentenced to life imprisonment without the possibility of parole in Michigan for the possession of half a pound of cocaine. The prosecutor had argued that, "In some respects, drug dealers are worse than murderers."[5] The Supreme Court apparently agreed.

In 1991, according to a private organization called the Sentencing Project, the United States had an incarceration rate of 426 per 100,000 population, compared to 333 for South Africa, 268 for the Soviet Union, 120 for Northern Ireland and less than 100 for any other developed country.[6] Including those on probation or parole, about 5 percent of American men are "under correctional supervision."[7]

THE INCENTIVE STRUCTURE

The war on drugs offers perverse incentives to all comers. To young people, especially minority males, it offers:

— More money than they can expect to earn any other way
— More sexual opportunities than they can obtain any other way
— More respect from peers and from strangers than they can obtain any other way
— Easy access to drugs, weapons, cars and other luxury goods
— An exciting and glamorous way of life

To law enforcement agents, it offers:

— Opportunities for personal and collective advancement
— An inexhaustible supply of suspects

— Opportunities for illicit profit
— Easy access to drugs, weapons, cars and other luxury goods
— An exciting and glamorous way of life

To professional criminals and criminal organizations, it offers:

— Larger profits than are available from any other kind of criminal activity
— Opportunities for organizational development
— Opportunities for manipulating the justice system

To the farmers in exotic lands who grow opium, coca and marijuana for export to the United States, it offers:

— More profit than they can obtain from any legal crop

RECENT TRENDS

Most of the recent increase in the correctional population oc-curred in years when violent crime was stable or declining. A great surge in crimes against the person occurred between 1967 and 1975 when the number of murders, rapes, robberies and aggravated assaults reported to the police went from 253 per 100,000 residents to 482, an increase of 91 percent in only 8 years. In the 16 years between 1975 and 1991, the number went from 482 to 758, an increase of 57 percent; most of this increase occurred between 1987 and 1991. The murder rate was at about the same level in 1991 as in 1975, robbery and rape had each increased by about 25 percent, but aggravated assault had doubled. Rates of property crimes more than doubled from 1965 to 1975; since then, the total rate has been approximately level.[8]

The foregoing trends are based on the Uniform Crime Reports of the FBI, a statistical series that is not entirely trustworthy. The information on trends in crime obtained from victimization sur-veys, beginning with the National Opinion Research Center (NORC) survey of 1965–66, and continuing with the National Crime Survey conducted annually by the Department of Justice since 1973, is believed to be more accurate. Robbery, rape, personal theft and household crimes all show modest declines from 1975 to

1990, according to this source.[9] Robbery is considered to be the best indicator of essential criminality because almost all robberies are committed by strangers and almost all are reported to the police.

Neither series is entirely reliable. The FBI figures are assembled from the unverified reports of thousands of police departments, many of which have motives for falsifying the numbers. The victimization surveys are subject to sampling errors and respondent bias. But several firm conclusions emerge from these shaky statistics: (1) the widespread public perception that all types of crime have been sharply rising is mistaken, (2) the incarceration mania of the 1980s began after the rise in crime rates had slackened and (3) the incarceration mania has not had any perceptible effect on the incidence of violent crimes.

The increase in prison commitments for drug offenses is largely responsible for the huge increase in the prison population, but there are other reasons as well. The operations of the criminal justice system are subject to marked oscillations. Although police efficiency, measured by the ratio of arrests to serious crimes, has not changed much since 1975,[10] prosecutorial efficiency, measured by the probability that an arrested person will be convicted, has gone sharply upward, along with the ratio of prison commitments to convictions and, in many jurisdictions, the average length of sentences.[11]

Americans have always been more prone to crime than the citizens of other developed countries,[12] but with large variations over time. The previous peak occurred in the mid-1920s, when per capita rates of homicide and other violent crimes were somewhat higher than they are today.[13]

The ethnic aspect of the incarceration mania is inescapable. At the end of 1988, blacks were 46 percent of male prisoners, 45 percent of female prisoners, 43 percent of jail inmates, 45 percent of parolees and 41 percent of incarcerated juveniles. Hispanics made up about 15 percent of these categories.[14]

According to current estimates, 13 percent of the U.S. population is black, that is, has any discernible trace of African ancestry. They are thus overrepresented in the prisoner population by a ratio of nearly 4 to 1. How much of this overrepresentation is attributable to discriminatory treatment in the criminal justice system is a long-debated and still unsettled question.[15] Victimization surveys attribute fewer than a third of crimes of violence to black offenders, but this showing is largely due to the great number of assaults by whites against whites. Regardless of the race of the victims, more robberies are attributed to blacks than to whites.[16] The victimization surveys do not provide comparable information on homicide.

The overrepresentation of Hispanics in the correctional population—less than 2 to 1—is serious but probably manageable. The overrepresentation of blacks is a demographic catastrophe. In 1990, the Senate Committee on Banking, Housing and Urban Affairs sponsored the creation of the 21st Century Commission on African-American Males, which publicized the chilling statistic that 25 percent of black men in the 25 to 29 age group were in prison, on probation or on parole, and described them as an endangered species.[17]

The incarceration mania is deplorable for many other reasons. American prisons damage their inmates by physical and psychological abuse, mostly from other prisoners; by encouraging drug habits; by strengthening criminal associations; and by imposing irremovable stigmas. They rarely rehabilitate or reform.

Three out of four serious offenders sentenced to prison terms have had previous convictions.[18] A study of a sample of offenders released from state prisons in 11 states in 1983 and followed for three years showed that the 63 percent of them who were rearrested within three years accumulated an average of 4.8 new charges.[19]

These extraordinarily high rates of recidivism are largely attributable to the lack of job opportunities for ex-convicts. Most employers refuse to hire them. There are no statutes that forbid discrimination against ex-convicts. There are no work release programs that amount to anything. A man coming out of prison usually finds himself unemployable and *persona non grata* in the law-abiding world. He has, in the usual case, no alternative but to rejoin the criminal underworld.

Many state prisons and local jails are awash in drugs.[20] Most of the people arrested, most of the people who serve time in prison or jail, most of the people released from prison or jail, are drug users. A federal study team that requested a voluntary interview and urinalysis from persons arrested for any cause in 22 cities in 1989 obtained astonishing results. More than 50 percent of all the arrestees, male and female, tested positive for illegal drugs at the time of arrest. More than 70 percent of both the men arrested in New York and Philadelphia and the women arrested in Washington, D.C., tested positive for cocaine alone.[21] A 1990 survey of jail inmates found that more than 75 percent of them had used illegal drugs.[22] Although there are no hard data on the availability of drugs in prisons or jails, the anecdotal evidence is overwhelming. The correctional process itself is a major factor contributing to drug use and prisoners who enter a correctional facility without a drug habit are likely to acquire one there.

Prisons are very expensive to build and operate: At current prices it costs about $300 million to construct a maximum security prison of average size and up to $60,000 per inmate per year to operate one.

The conventional purposes of incarceration are rehabilitation, deterrence, prevention and retribution. The U.S. criminal justice system, as we know it, has given up on rehabilitation. What about the other objectives?

Deterrence—whereby other potential offenders are discouraged by the punishment of an apprehended offender—is difficult, indeed impossible, to measure in the field. But experiments in social psychology laboratories suggest that punishment has a deterrent effect if it is (1) quick and (2) certain. If punishment is unpredictable or separated from the offense in time, it is unlikely to achieve much deterrence.[23]

One of the most significant changes in the criminal justice system in recent decades has been the prolongation of the interval between arrest and conviction and between conviction and sentencing and the further lapse of time for appeals after sentencing. Between arrest and conviction, there is enough time, in thousands of cases, for the accused to go out and commit new offenses.[24] And in the case of very serious offenses, a conviction is *never* the final disposition. Capital murder cases, with all their procedural safeguards, commonly take more than a decade to resolve.

It was not always so. In earlier times, most felony cases were resolved in less than a week. Today, the average interval is close to a year.[25] We ostensibly use the same procedures but they work very differently now.

Defense lawyers say that these delays protect innocent people charged with crimes they did not commit. There is a small grain of truth in that argument but most of the procedural delays in the justice system have nothing to do with a search for buried truth. They are inefficiencies that have hardened into custom because they are convenient for lawyers and judges, and they have the incidental effect of making the truth more elusive as witnesses disappear and memories fade.

The question of whether the death penalty is an effective deterrent becomes altogether meaningless when the facts are considered. Death sentences in the United States are not what they seem. At the beginning of 1989, for example, there were 2,117 prisoners in this country under sentence of death and during that year, 251 more were added. A total of 16 were executed—fewer than 1 percent of those under sentence.[26] Being condemned to death in the United States is somewhat more life-threatening than downhill skiing but much less dangerous than hang-gliding.

The function of prevention is not much better served by the existing system. As with the death penalty, prison terms are exaggerated to reassure a public that is forever urging its representatives to get tough on crime. Sentences to prison typically far exceed the length of time actually served, which is almost always shortened by reductions for good behavior, by parole or by release for administrative convenience. The average sentence of felons to state prisons is about seven years; the average time served is about two years.

A very high proportion of serious crimes are committed by a small number of high-frequency offenders so that, if it were possible to identify and sequester them, a significant reduction of crime rates might be achieved. Attempts in a few states to identify high-frequency offenders have had some limited success. Statutes that set mandatory higher sentences for repeat offenders are clumsy instruments for the purpose, since many high-frequency offenders do not have long arrest records. They are more easily identified by interview than by the operations of the justice system.

The other purpose that incarceration is supposed to serve is retribution—the infliction of pain to match the pain caused by the crime. Unhappily, the pain of incarceration in an American prison under current conditions is greatest for the inmates who have inflicted the least pain on others: check forgers, drug-using students and other nonviolent offenders are the ones likely to suffer the most pain in prison, while the streetwise, violent offender can make a better adjustment there. Another peculiarity of the American correctional system is that we impose longer sentences for common crimes than any other developed country. Even the fractions of sentences that are actually served are much longer that the sentences for similar offenses in Western European countries, where deprivation of freedom for a year or two is regarded as a severe punishment. Although we pretend that our prison sentences are much longer than they are, they still exceed the sentences that would be regarded elsewhere as appropriate retribution.

And, as previously noted, the demand for retribution against drug offenders is not restricted by any notion of a rough balance between the pain of the victim and the pain of the offender. The victim is conceived to be society itself and the offense as unforgivable as high treason or witchcraft. At a 1991 crime summit, the U.S. attorney general seemed to identify drug trafficking as the principal cause of violent crime:

Drug trafficking and its inevitable handmaiden of violence are the greatest threats to what I have always called the first civil right of every American—the right to be free from fear in our homes, on our streets, and in our communities.[27]

Empirically, the direct effects of the illegal drugs on health and behavior are clearly less harmful than the indirect effects of the effort to suppress them. Some vehicular and industrial accidents are attributable to marijuana intoxication but the rate is low. Addiction to heroin, methadone, morphine and other narcotics is frequently incapacitating and disturbing to family relationships but it is not especially conducive to violent behavior. Many addicts eventually abandon the addiction without treatment. The behavioral changes induced by cocaine vary unpredictably from mild to incapacitating. Some infants are damaged neurologically by the cocaine habits of their mothers, but the damage may not be permanent.

The deleterious effects of alcohol and tobacco are enormously greater than those of the illegal drugs. At the highest estimate, illegal drugs may account for as many as 3,000 deaths a year in the

United States, excluding AIDS cases contracted by sharing needles.[28] By contrast, the National Centers for Disease Control estimated that 105,000 Americans died in 1987 from the direct effects of alcohol, about a third from drunken injuries and the remainder from alcohol-induced diseases such as cirrhosis of the liver.[29] Lung cancer and other obstructive pulmonary diseases highly correlated with tobacco smoking cause about 150,000 deaths every year; cardiovascular diseases, also closely associated with smoking, cause almost a million more.[30]

But the chariots of the war on drugs roll on. Unlike the prohibition experiment of the 1920s, which began with a single legislative act, the war on drugs evolved gradually out of futile and uncoordinated efforts to suppress the consumption of heroin by inner-city youths in the 1950s, of marijuana by an entire adolescent generation in the 1960s, and of hallucinogens by the cultural leaders of that generation.

As enforcement efforts drove prices up, dealing in drugs became wonderfully profitable for everybody concerned, from the original farmers and processors to the importers and wholesale distributors down to the amateur dealer on the street corner. Everybody made money, and lots of money. It got better and better as enforcement intensified and new products entered the market. Cocaine came along in the late 1970s and crack cocaine ten years later. The cocaine market mushroomed in a few years from nothing at all to something like $100 billion in annual sales.[31]

Meanwhile a peculiar mechanism evolved whereby the schools and the mass media cooperate in promoting the sale of illegal drugs. Their efforts are not intended as advertising but they serve the purpose. Both the drug education programs in the schools and the drug coverage of the mass media emphasize in a shameless way the irresistible character of these substances—how seductive they are, how difficult to reject, how a single puff can create a lifelong addiction and so on. The unintended result is to make these products particularly attractive to restless young people. Moreover, both drug education efforts and mass media coverage of the war against drugs provide a great deal of technical information to potential users—how the products are produced, where they can be obtained, how much they cost and how to self-administer them. If there is an American adolescent who is not fully informed about the desired effects of illegal drugs, he or she has been shockingly inattentive in school.

THE SEARCH FOR SOLUTIONS

The only way out of this morass is to legalize the importation, production and sale of the drugs that are now banned. This would do away with the extraordinary profits that drug traffickers now enjoy, end the boom in prison construction and enable the criminal justice system to refocus on crime control.

What makes this scenario plausible is that so many kinds of harmful intoxication in this country are regulated with only occasional recourse to the criminal justice system—not only alcohol, tobacco and caffeine but analgesics, tranquilizers, stimulants, antidepressants, barbiturates and mood-changing drugs prescribed legally and circulated illegally to tens of millions of users. Many of them have more harmful side effects than heroin or cocaine.

But the obstacles to legalization are formidable. Public opinion favors severity over tolerance by wide margins. The hundreds of thousands of law enforcement agents enlisted in the war on drugs are not interested in a cease-fire. Neither are the producers and the dealers. As a practical matter, it would very difficult to dismantle the maze of federal, state, local and foreign legislation created to deal with drug abuse.

The principal argument against legalization is that it would increase the consumption of the substances that are now banned. And indeed it might. The repeal of alcohol prohibition in 1933 did not, so far as the imperfect record goes, reduce the per capita consumption of alcohol, although the speakeasy and the neighborhood bootlegger disappeared and the beer barons retired.

The long-run effects of legalization on usage are quite impossible to predict. When narcotics were freely available around the turn of the century, the relative number of addicts was about the same as now, but most of them were elderly middle-class white people, and addiction was almost unknown among adolescents. Marijuana, which is still widely available today, seems to have passed its peak among young people, who have always been the principal users; although there are signs of a comeback. Cocaine, and then crack cocaine, were the first illegal drugs to generate a true mass market. It is unlikely that their use would contract with legalization. As to the hallucinogens and stimulants that come and go with the style changes of the illegal drug market, their potential volume after legalization might depend upon whether they were allowed enough paid promotion to make up for the loss of the free promotion they now get from drug education programs and from the media.

As with alcohol, the legalization of drugs would not imply deregulation. Sale to minors would surely be prohibited and the distribution of adulterated or toxic products would be penalized—something that is not done today. Careful labelling would be required, as with other pharmaceuticals. Drug advertising would presumably be excluded from the mass media much as cigarette advertising is banned from television. Again on the example of alcohol and tobacco, drug products should be taxed, but not so heavily as to provoke the development of a black market.

Enterprises and institutions would surely be allowed to restrict and to penalize drug use. The use of drugs might reasonably be banned on common carriers, in schools, in workplaces and in restaurants and shops, much as smoking is banned in many places of public assembly today. And, of course, the operation of vehicles or machinery under the influence of drugs would be handled in the same way as the much larger problem of driving or operating machinery under the influence of alcohol.

None of these measures would inflate the prices or increase the appeal of drugs in the ways that the current efforts at repression do. None of them would sustain the existing roles of blacks and Hispanics in the drug market or the resulting stereotypes of drug users.

Legalization will disable the motor that drives both the expansion of the criminal underworld and the incarceration mania. But it will not resolve the accumulated ills of the past 20 years. The connection between violent crime and drug use that has been established by ill-considered policies will continue for years before it weakens. The population of nearly unemployable ex-prisoners will continue to generate high social costs even after the prison population begins to shrink. The prisons and jails will still, at least for a while, be awash in drugs, either because they are no longer prohibited and can be obtained freely by habitual users or because institutional prohibition raises their local prices enough to make dealing profitable.

But since the present trends are insupportable, legalization must occur sooner or later. The often suggested alternatives of drug treatment and education do not touch the central mechanism, whereby efforts to repress drug use create perverse incentives for dealers, users and enforcement agents at all levels. Drug treatment can only be effective with willing clients, who are always a small minority of users, while drug education, as we have seen, is as likely to promote as to discourage drug abuse.

A secondary approach to ending the incarceration mania is to reconsider incarceration itself. From every standpoint, the typical term of imprisonment in an American prison is a bad bargain for society. It costs a great deal and is unlikely to improve the future behavior of the offender.

Under the pressure of overcrowding, correction officials in the federal system and in several of the states have developed a variety of programs to reduce the time spent behind bars by sentenced offenders.[32] In some jurisdictions, fines and restitution can be substituted for imprisonment in the case of employable first offenders.

A few states have experimented with "boot camps" for young male prisoners. These are quasi-military units in rural settings. They feature close order drill, strenuous exercise, unit solidarity and strict discipline. The effect on recidivism has been inconclusive.

In many jurisdictions and in the federal system, some offenders are confined in halfway houses and other community facilities. But this treatment is usually reserved for prisoners approaching the end of their sentences.

House arrest is an arrangement in which prisoners are confined in their own homes, with or without permission for approved sorties. In Florida and some other states, house arrest is enforced by electronic surveillance. A device is attached to the prisoner that continuously transmits his or her exact location to a central monitor.

The most promising of these measures appears to be closely supervised probation, as advocated by the National Council on Crime and Delinquency and actually practiced in Florida, Delaware, Oregon, New Jersey and a few other jurisdictions. In one form of closely supervised probation, convicted nonviolent offenders serve the first few months of their sentences in prison and are then sent back home, where they are placed under the supervision of a probation officer who is responsible for only 20 or so cases and maintains close contact with all of them. The probationer can work and lead a normal life, subject to a strict set of rules concerning criminal contacts, drug and alcohol use, and so forth. Those who obey the rules serve out the remainder of their sentences in this peaceable way and are then released. Those who break the rules are returned to prison immediately.

The principal flaw in this arrangement is the excessive personal power it gives to the probation officer but due process can be restored by a subsequent review of every revoked probation. Closely supervised probation is expensive compared to ordinary, carelessly supervised probation, but dirt cheap compared to imprisonment.

So far, there is no firm evidence that any of these alternatives to incarceration reduce recidivism, but it quite certain that they do not increase it. The initiative for experimentation has come in most instances from corrections officials trying to cope with prison overcrowding. Meanwhile, Congress, state legislatures and courts continue to raise the punitive ante. Testifying before a congressional committee, the Commissioner of Corrections of Delaware observed:

They have just enacted, for instance—if a person which in the past would just be a user, five grams of cocaine, that has been redefined under the Delaware Code as a trafficker in drugs, getting a 3–year mandatory prison sentence. The consequence is that, our prosecutors tell us, instead of none of those people being received in prison, we may get as high as 70 a month.[33]

At the same 1989 hearing, the director of the Federal Bureau of Prisons, whose system was then operating at 159 percent of its rated capacity, noted that the proportion of drug offenders in the federal prison population had risen from 25 percent in 1981 to 47 percent in 1989 and was expected to reach 70 percent within five or six years.[34]

The war on drugs is both the direct and the indirect cause of the incarceration mania. Directly, it accounts for much of the growth in the prison population. Indirectly, the frustrations of drug enforcement have fueled the public demand for harsher sentencing of all offenders.

The public has come to believe that the drug problem can be fixed by forceful police action. The available evidence suggests that forceful police action is largely responsible for the drug problem as we know it.

The public has come to believe that violent crime is on the rise and can only be curbed by catching more criminals and imprisoning them for longer terms. The available evidence indicates that violent crime has been declining moderately and that long prison sentences probably do more to increase than to decrease it. As of 1994, the leading proposal in state legislatures and Congress for reforming the criminal justice system was some form of "three strikes and out"—a mandatory life sentence or a very long sentence for a third violent crime, or a second violent crime, or just a third felony conviction. These ingenious schemes may eventually crowd the country's prisons with elderly inmates who, if they were still on the outside, would be quite harmless, since violent crime is virtually monopolized by youths and young men.

The promise to be tough on crime has been incorporated in the litany of electoral campaigning. The memory of Willie Horton still warns off candidates who might be tempted to omit that part of the ritual. And once returned to office, it is difficult for them to take any position that might open them to the accusation of being soft about law enforcement.

This conflict between public opinion and the current realities of the criminal justice system may be the most intractable of all the problems faced by our five failing systems. The incarceration mania cannot be halted unless the war on drugs is wound up first. But most of our fellow citizens and most of our elected officials firmly support that misguided war and are quite blind to its self-defeating character.

The only bright spot in this dismal picture is the precedent of the alcohol prohibition experiment, which once enjoyed widespread public support but was abandoned quickly and quietly when the public mood changed. The circumstances are not exactly

parallel, since the proportion of illicit drinkers in the 1933 population was higher than the proportion of illicit drug users in the 1993
population, and the Irish and Italian Americans associated with
illegal alcohol were never viewed with as much distaste as the
African Americans and Puerto Ricans associated with illegal drugs.
On the other hand, the adverse effects of the first prohibition
experiment were almost insignificant compared with the horren-
dous consequences of the second. There is room for hope.

NOTES

1. U.S. Bureau of Justice Statistics: *Prisons and Prisoners in the United
States*, NCJ-137002 (1992); *Correctional Populations in the United States 1988*,
NCJ-124280, *Prisoners 1925–1981* (1982); *National Update* 1, no. 3, NCJ-
133097 (January 1992).

2 U.S. Bureau of Justice Statistics, "Prisoners in 1991," by Tracy L.
Morton and Danielle C. Morton (May 1992).

3. U.S. Bureau of Justice Statistics, *National Update* 1, no. 3 (January
1992).

4. The story is told at length in "Drug Wars: High in the Andes," *The
Economist* 326, no. 7798 (February 13, 1993): 45–46.

5. Ruth Marcus, "Life in Prison for Cocaine Possession," *Washington
Post* (November 5, 1990): A1, A8.

6. Sharon LaFraniere, "U.S. Has Most Prisoners Per Capita in the
World," *Washington Post* (January 5, 1991): A3.

7. Curiously, the relatively small (about 20,000) population of juvenile detention facilities hardly grew at all between 1974 and 1985, although juvenile offenders account for a large share of crime against
persons and property. U.S. Bureau of Justice Statistics, *Report to the Nation
on Crime and Justice*, 2d ed. (1988), 105.

8. *Statistical Abstract of the United States 1979* (hereafter *SAUS*), Table
197; *SAUS93*, Table 300.

9. U.S. Bureau of Justice Statistics: *Criminal Victimization in the United
States, 1973–1990 Trends* (1991); *Violent Crime in the United States*, NCJ-
127855 (1991).

10. There was a steady decline in police clearance rates from 1961,
when there were 654 arrests for every 1,000 violent offenses (murder,
rape, robbery, aggravated assault) reported to the police, to 1974, when
there were only 452. Since then, there has been no significant change. The
1990 rate was 439. The ratio of prison commitments to arrests for serious
offenses also declined from 1960 to 1974, from 16 percent to 10 percent;
then it rose again to an average of 14 percent in the 1980s. Based on U.S.

Bureau of Justice Statistics: *Prisoners in 1986* (1987); *Sourcebook of Criminal Statistics 1991* (1992); "Prisoners in 1991" by Morton and Morton.

11. For example, the average length of sentence for violators convicted in federal district courts went from 38 months in 1972 to 59 months in 1990. U.S. Bureau of Justice Statistics, *Sourcebook of Criminal Statistics 1990*, NCJ-130580 (1991).

12. Although it is interesting to note that when all causes of unnatural death (homicide, suicide, accidents) are taken into account, the United States is only a little more violent than Switzerland and a little less violent than France. "Economic and Financial Indicators," *The Economist* 326, no. 7794 (January 16, 1993): 107.

13. U.S. Bureau of Justice Statistics: *Violent Crime*, 6.

14. U.S. Bureau of Justice Statistics, BJS Data Report 1989, NCJ-121514 (1990).

15. For a summary of the literature on this question, see Robert M. O'Brien, "The Interracial Nature of Violent Crimes: A Reexamination," *American Journal of Sociology* 92, no. 4 (1987): 817–835.

16. U.S. Bureau of Justice Statistics, *Criminal Victimization in the United States 1990*, NCJ-134126 (1992), Tables 48 and 52.

17. The statistics are incomplete and not altogether reliable, but the earliest national data, for 1926, gives the black percentage of state prison admissions as 23 percent. By 1974, it had risen to approximately the present level. The crisis reflects the recent growth of the correctional population, not of the black share of that population. See U.S. Bureau of Justice Statistics, *Race of Prisoners Admitted to State and Federal Institutions 1926–1986*, NCJ-125618 (1991).

18. U.S. Bureau of Justice Statistics, *BJS Data Report 1989*.

19. U.S. Bureau of Justice Statistics, *Violent Crime in the United States; Prisons and Prisoners in the United States*.

20. A 1989 study of jail inmates found that "A majority of those who used a major drug regularly began regular use after their first arrest." U.S. Bureau of Justice Statistics, *Drugs and Jail Inmates 1989*, Special Report (1989), 7.

21. U.S. Bureau of Justice Statistics, *NIJ Reports*, no. 221 (1990).

22. U.S. Bureau of Justice Statistics, *National Update* 1, no. 2, NCJ-131778 (October 1991).

23. See Nehemia Friedland, "The Combined Effect of Severity and the Certainty of Threatened Penalties: Additive or Interactive?" *Journal of Applied Social Psychology* 20 (September 1990):1358–68.

24. In a large sample of felony defendants drawn from the nation's 75 most populous counties in 1988, nearly two-thirds were released into the community pending disposition of their cases; 18 percent of these were arrested for a new felony while on release and two-thirds of these were

released again. U.S. Bureau of Justice Statistics, *National Update* 1, no. 1, NCJ-129863 (July 1991).

25. I have not been able to find national data earlier than 1970 but we discovered in the Middletown III study of Muncie, Indiana, that the average interval between arrest and final disposition in criminal cases increased from 6 days in 1925 to more than 12 months in 1976. The national average is currently about 10 months. U.S. Bureau of Justice Statistics, *Felony Sentences in State Courts 1988* (1990): Table 11.

26. U.S. Bureau of Justice Statistics, *Capital Punishment* 1989 (1990).

27. Dick Thornburgh, quoted on the cover page of U.S. Bureau of Justice Statistics, *Violent Crime in the United States*.

28. Estimated from *SAUS93*, Table 135.

29. Associated Press report (March 23, 1990).

30. *SAUS93*, Table 126.

31. A 1989 estimate by the United States Chamber of Commerce.

32. An excellent account of these innovations can be found in U.S. Congress, House, Committee on the Judiciary, *Oversight Hearings on Corrections: Overcrowding and Alternatives to Incarceration*, Serial No. 59 (1990).

33. Ibid., testimony of Commissioner Watson, 130.

34. Ibid., 3.

7

THE COMPENSATION OF INJURIES

CAUSES AND CONSEQUENCES

The root causes of the crisis in the American system for compensating injuries are certain legal procedures that are unique to the United States: the use of juries to settle intricate technical questions and to assess damages, the absence of guidelines for calculating damages, the payment of plaintiffs' lawyers by contingency fees, and reliance on partisan expert witnesses.

Life in an industrial society is hazardous. (Life in a preindustrial society is even more hazardous, but the causes of harm are simpler.) In the United States, as in other advanced nations, millions of people are killed or injured in automobile, industrial and home accidents. Millions more are injured by medical treatment and athletics. Some are struck down by corrosive chemicals or contaminated food. Some contract fatal diseases after exposure to radioactivity, or to toxic substances such as tobacco or contaminated blood.

In the United States, people who suffer bodily or mental injury from external causes are encouraged to find someone, preferably an affluent person or corporation, who can be held responsible for the injury and made to pay damages. Prior to the 1960s, the injured person had to show that the irresponsible conduct of the person or corporation from whom damages were claimed was a direct cause of the injury. Employees injured on the job were covered by a special arrangement called workers' compensation, which disregarded the question of fault and required employers to pay for lost wages and medical expenses. In other cases of personal injury, caused by defective products and dangerous conditions, careless or malicious actions, or incompetent medical care, the law allowed the victim to recover reasonable damages if it could be shown that the victim had done nothing wrong and the other party was at fault.

Beginning in the 1960s state and federal courts in the United States began to change both sides of this formula and to allow damage suits when (1) the plaintiff had not taken reasonable care to prevent the injury or (2) the defendant *had* taken reasonable care. This change has often been described as a legal revolution. According to one critic:

Prior to the revolution, negligence was defined with reference to deviations from normally accepted behavior. After the revolution, however, the ambitions of the law were different, to internalize injury costs and to provide compensation insurance to injured victims, especially the poor.[1]

The revolution was begun by a school of legal economists who theorized that the social costs of the unavoidable risks associated with technology should be borne by large enterprises and not by individuals. In 1964, this doctrine, in the form of "strict liability," was embodied in the Second Restatement of Torts by the prestigious American Law Institute, and it was subsequently adopted by legislation in 48 of the 50 states.

The liability system is less centralized than health care, education, welfare or criminal justice. There is no federal department of liability and statistics for the system as a whole are hard to come by. But as in the other failing systems, the redesign accomplished since 1960 by legislative and judicial action has been plainly counterproductive. The system's monetary costs are staggering and it has created a gamut of serious problems that are unique to the United States. In every other developed country, personal injuries are compensated more efficiently and equitably than here.[2]

For convenient description, the liability system can be divided into six fields. Each field is inefficient but some are more inefficient than others. In approximate order of inefficiency, they involve the liability of:

— Manufacturers and merchants for injuries by their products
— Polluters for environmental injuries
— Health care providers for injuries to their patients
— Landowners and municipalities for injuries on their property
— Employers for work-related injuries and diseases
— Vehicle drivers and owners for traffic accidents

This is not a complete catalog, but it covers most of the system.[3]

THE INCENTIVE STRUCTURE

The liability system offers a rich selection of perverse incentives to all of its players.

There are perverse incentives for claimants:

— To seek compensation for exaggerated and imaginary injuries
— To set extravagant values on their injuries
— To seek dual compensation for losses already compensated

There are perverse incentives for providers:

— To increase prices disproportionately
— To discontinue useful activities and products
— To avoid innovation

There are perverse incentives for plaintiffs' lawyers:

— To inflate the dollar value of the claims they represent
— To take an excessive share of compensation payments
— To obfuscate factual and scientific issues
— To promote and settle nuisance suits

There are perverse incentives for insurers:

— To set unreasonable rates
— To skim their markets
— To withdraw coverage of essential activities

PRODUCT LIABILITY

Every one of these perverse incentives is conspicuous in the burgeoning field of product liability. Before the liability revolution, the manufacturer of a defective item was held responsible for any injuries it caused in normal use. Defective items—contaminated food products, machines with missing parts— were taken as proof of failures in the production process. The producer's responsibility for such failures was clear. Most of the claims arising from product defects were promptly settled out of court, as they still are today.

But the liability revolution added two new kinds of product liability: defective design and failure to warn.

A jury can now find that the design of a product is defective and dangerous even if the manufacturer has complied with all of the applicable standards for products of that type, and even if the weight of evidence indicates that the product is safe when properly used. Thus, the design of light airplanes is tightly regulated by the Federal Aviation Administration (FAA), which will not certify a given model as airworthy until it has passed a long series of inspections and flight tests, and does not allow a plane to fly unless it is continually serviced according to FAA requirements. Every plane crash is closely investigated by the National Transportation Safety Board and/or the FAA, who attempt to determine the cause.

But between 1978 and 1988, the U.S. light aircraft industry, formerly the strongest in the world, was effectively put out of business by personal injury lawsuits. The annual production of planes dropped by 94 percent as product liability insurance was first priced to astronomical levels and then became unavailable at any price.[4]

There were no significant changes in the number of accidents during that period but the volume of litigation increased tenfold. It became standard practice for the relatives of people killed in light plane crashes to sue the manufacturer, alleging that defective design had caused the crash. Many juries accepted that theory and assessed heavy damages against the manufacturers.[5]

In almost every such case, the courts brushed aside the findings of expert investigators that the crash was due to pilot error or other causes in favor of the jury's opinion that it was due to defective design. The fact that the manufacturer had complied with all of the FAA regulations concerning design, manufacture and testing was not allowed as evidence of good design. Indeed, some plaintiffs' lawyers argued ingeniously that compliance with the regulations showed that the manufacturer was trying to do as little as possible to make the product safe. An English underwriter explained why Lloyds insurers withdrew from this market. "We are quite prepared," he said, "to insure against the risks of aviation, but not the risks of the American legal system."

A frequent cause of light plane crashes is carburetor icing, which can usually be prevented by the pilot's timely application of carburetor heat. Private pilot training emphasizes this danger and the procedures for dealing with it. There is no practical way to eliminate the possibility of carburetor icing in light single-engine aircraft without adding excessive weight and complexity, thus creating other hazards. But juries that did not include any pilots or engineers were often persuaded to think otherwise and to pile punitive damages on top of the compensatory damages assessed against manufacturers. Under the new liability doctrine, it made no difference if the defense could show that the pilot had neglected to apply carburetor heat when it was called for.

The negative social effects of this litigation went beyond the ruin of the manufacturers. What remained of the new plane market was taken over by less regulated foreign manufacturers, while old planes that would formerly have been scrapped were patched up and kept in service, to the detriment of safety. Product research and innovation in this field came to a full stop.

The devastation of the general aviation industry was the extreme case, but dozens of other industries suffered to a lesser degree from the liability revolution. People who lose their balance and fall off ladders now routinely sue the ladder maker, who does not dare to introduce new safety features. The makers and sellers of power tools, household appliances, garden equipment, toys, sleepwear, champagne and pesticides, among many others, are wary of introducing new products or improving old ones. Some useful pharmaceutical products are no longer available at all because plaintiffs won large awards against their manufacturers on the thinnest of scientific evidence.[6] Product liability premiums add several hundred dollars to the production cost of an American automobile—an expense unknown to foreign automakers.[7]

In February 1993, a jury in Atlanta, Georgia, awarded $4.2 million in compensatory damages and $101 million in punitive damages to the parents of a Georgia teen-ager who died in a high-speed crash involving a pickup truck manufactured by General Motors. The jurors may have been influenced by a segment aired on NBC's "Dateline" in November 1992, which alleged that a design defect in GM trucks with external fuel tanks made them likely to burn on impact. Shortly after the verdict it turned out that the NBC program had faked its evidence, using incendiary devices to cause a fire after a staged collision and attributing the fire to the rupture of a tank that actually remained intact. NBC apologized, GM appealed the Atlanta verdict, and the drama rolled merrily on.[8] More than four million similar trucks are on the road and hundreds of other suits have been settled or are pending.

The case exemplifies the peculiar features of the liability system as it operates today. As usual, compliance with all applicable government regulations and industry standards is no defense against an allegation of defective design. As usual, juries have no difficulty with problems of causation. The plaintiff died when his truck was hit squarely on the driver's door by another vehicle going 70 miles an hour, but the jury was sure that he was not killed by the impact. The most peculiar feature of the system is that juries are given no guidelines for calculating damages. This jury decided that the young man's life was worth $4.2 million to his parents. In the absence of any standard, it could as easily have set the figure at $42,000 or $42 million. It also thought that the parents should get $101 million to punish General Motors for its wicked conduct. No monetary standard was consulted to arrive at that figure[9] nor was there any rationale for awarding so great a windfall to the plaintiffs' lawyers, who stood to net about $35 million from this case if the verdict were sustained on appeal.

The liability revolution introduced another new basis for claims called "failure to warn." When no defects of either manufacture or design can be found in a product, it is still possible to construct a claim out of the manufacturers' failure to warn the consumer of a potential danger. It does not have to be a hidden danger. For purposes of litigation, the consumer is presumed to be a feckless idiot, incapable of perceiving the most obvious hazards without a written warning. The new doctrine has produced some of the most bizarre decisions in legal history.

A landmark New Jersey case involved a claim by a worker that an asbestos manufacturer should be liable for damages because the manufacturer had failed to warn the worker that asbestos could cause cancer. The manufacturer was able to prove that the relationship between asbestos and cancer was totally unknown at the time of the worker's employment. Nevertheless, the Supreme Court of New Jersey held that the manufacturer had breached its duty to warn the worker that asbestos caused cancer.[10]

In a Maryland suit brought by teen-age girls who were burned when they tried to make a scented candle by pouring cologne on a lighted candle, the manufacturer of the cologne was held liable for failure to warn that pouring the product on an open flame could cause a fire.[11]

In Missouri, a child was injured when the child's father left a lawn mower running and unattended. Despite warnings in the product pamphlet that said "Never Leave Equipment Unattended," "Keep Children or Pets Away," and "Always Shut Off Engine," the manufacturer was held liable for failing to warn that the mower might engage if left unattended.[12]

Chevron Chemical was sued in federal court by an employee who contracted pulmonary fibrosis, allegedly as the result of long-term exposure to a chemical called paraquat. The federal Environmental Protection Agency requires a label on this product warning, among other things, against "prolonged exposure" and "repeated contact." Chevron had put this label on the product. The company was held liable for a defective warning although the court acknowledged that Chevron had no legal right to change or supplement the warning prescribed by EPA.[13]

The defective warning doctrine enables product liability to be established and damages awarded even when no defect can be found in the product or its design or the instructions provided for its use. Since no warning can anticipate all the circumstances of a particular accident, any warning can be construed as defective if jurors and judges want to assign liability to an affluent defendant.

The legal theory behind these shenanigans holds that the expansion of product liability deters the production of unsafe products and shifts the risks of technology to those who can best afford to bear them. There is less to this argument than meets the eye. Against products that are demonstrably unsafe, the old liability system provided adequate protection. The new system mainly serves to deter the manufacture of products that comply with prevailing safety standards and that are not unsafe when properly used, as well as to discourage all types of product innovation, those that might enhance safety along with those that carry unknown risks. As one critic comments:

No liability rule, however harsh, can ever deter risk in itself; it can only deter behavior that gets people sued, which is not at all the same thing. . . . A drugmaker sued by patients who suffer a side effect reformulates the product at a lower and less effective dosage. An automaker sued because its seat belts let users add slack, thus reducing the belt's efficacy, does away with the slacking device—and some comfort-minded drivers start going beltless. Developers sued for negligent security after a mugging respond by avoiding multiple convenient exits in building designs— good for crime safety but bad for fire safety.[14]

Although deterrence is difficult to measure statistically, we know that overall U.S. rates of household, industrial and transportation accidents have been declining slowly and steadily for many years.[15] The vast growth of the liability system in recent years was not a response to an increase in the frequency or severity of personal injuries, nor has it had any perceptible effect on injury rates.

Shifting the burden of technological risk is a reasonable objective that the new liability system does not begin to accomplish, since most of its benefits go to lawyers and insurers rather than to claimants, and the compensation of claimants is slow, unpredictable and erratic. In very many cases, liability litigation merely shifts the burden of risk from one insurer to another while adding enormous overhead costs.[16]

ENVIRONMENTAL LIABILITY

In the list of liability sectors presented earlier in this chapter, which ranked the leading types of liability by their social inefficiency, I put environmental liability above medical malpractice liability because there are more claims for imaginary injuries in the former category. I put it below product liability because it seems to do less overall harm.

Environmental liability is an almost new field. It was inaugurated by the Love Canal furor of 1978 and flowered amazingly in the 1980s. Prior to that time, claims for personal injury from harmful releases into the environment (escaped wild beasts, poisonous effluents and so forth) were only actionable if the causal relationship was clear. In the new system, the causes of injuries are almost always unclear; the existence of injuries may be uncertain too. Neither condition is an obstacle to successful litigation.

The Love Canal was a tract of land in Niagara Falls, New York, that had been owned by a chemical company and used for the underground storage of toxic waste. It was acquired by the town in 1953 for the construction of a public school, apparently against the warnings of the original owners, and it later changed hands and was developed for single-family housing. When waste from the chemical dump seeped into these homes, the problem attracted wide attention. President Carter described it as a national emergency. It made the nation aware of the existence of other toxic waste sites and led directly to the enactment of the Superfund legislation in 1980.[17]

The original Superfund law[18] passed by Congress in 1980 established a $1.6 billion trust fund to clean up about 400 hazardous waste sites. Over the next few years the number of sites and the estimated costs of cleanup grew exponentially. By 1985, 10,000 sites had been identified and estimates of $100 billion were heard. In 1986, the cleanup fund was increased to $9 billion, but in 1987 the General Accounting Office estimated that there might be 425,000 sites and the cost might be as high as $1 trillion. The Superfund legislation established the principle of joint and several liability for the users of dumps. Users could be held liable even if they proved that their actions were prudent and nonnegligent. Private citizens and municipalities were authorized to sue presumed polluters on behalf of themselves and others. Several of the states passed similar legislation.

Litigators were not slow to respond to this lavish invitation. Huber lists 14 combined or class action suits alleging personal injury from toxic wastes filed between 1982 and 1986 that brought huge settlements or verdicts. The Agent Orange suit against Dow

Chemical Company enlisted 2.4 million plaintiffs and led to a $180 million verdict.[19]

The most striking feature of these cases was that none of the successful plaintiffs could prove that they had been injured by the pollutants in question. In every instance, the hypothesis that they had contracted disease or suffered physical injury from exposure to pollutants was speculative and unsupported by firm evidence. In environmental injury suits, Huber remarks:

Both sides are horrified at the prospect of taking matters to a jury. Plaintiffs fear that a jury might look at the facts carefully; defendants fear that it will not. The result has been a series of settlements detached from any objective measures of harm. Hundreds of millions of dollars have now changed hands in such settlements, but not one has involved evidence linking alleged cause and observed effect in a way that epidemiologists and public health experts in the mainstream scientific community consider close to convincing.[20]

Given the loose standards of proof in environmental liability cases and the potentially huge awards, it has become almost impossible to obtain insurance against environmental liability, although the Superfund legislation requires companies involved in cleanup operations to carry such insurance. This impasse is one of several reasons why the Superfund cleanup has been a fiasco. In addition, an astonishing proportion of Superfund money has been spent on "administrative expenses," rather than on actually cleaning up hazardous waste.

MEDICAL MALPRACTICE LIABILITY

Medical malpractice liability is differently configured than other fields of the liability system. Claimants must prove that they were injured by the negligence of a health care provider in the course of treatment; there has been no shift to strict liability here. Unlike other kinds of liability insurance, most malpractice insurance is not experience-rated, so that losing a case does not affect the future premiums of an insured defendant.

Nevertheless, medical malpractice liability is afflicted by desperate problems. The number of claims and the size of awards have skyrocketed over the past 25 years.[21] For some physicians and hospitals malpractice premiums increased by more than 20,000 percent during that period. Thousands of obstetricians and nurse-midwives have quit practice to avoid malpractice liability, creating a shortage of birth attendants in many places.[22] The fear of malpractice suits is pervasive and acute throughout the medical community. A great deal of testing and treatment is apparently inflicted on patients for the sole purpose of reducing malpractice liability. This is called "defensive medicine" and it is said to add many unnecessary billions to the nation's health care bill. At the same time, promising treatments are commonly withheld from patients if they involve unknown malpractice risks.[23] The doctor-patient relationship is probably more troubled in the United States today than anywhere else in the world; some doctors regard every patient as a potential litigant. The doctor-lawyer relationship has become extraordinarily bitter. Doctors complain incessantly that the greed and chicanery of lawyers is responsible for the malpractice crisis. Lawyers insist that medical incompetence is the reason. There is some merit to both accusations.

Prior to 1965, there were very few suits for medical malpractice in the United States and most of them were unsuccessful, since physicians customarily refused to testify against each other, and it was considered unethical for nurses to testify against physicians. This changed during the ideological turmoil of the 1960s when rebellious factions appeared in the medical community and made testimony available to claimants. Between 1965 and 1970, as many malpractice claims were filed as during the previous half century, and the number has continued to grow. National statistics are scanty, but it appears that between 1970 and 1990, the number of malpractice claims increased by a factor of 10, the average settlement by somewhat more and the cost of malpractice insurance by much more. A neurosurgeon practicing in New Jersey in 1990 would be charged an annual premium of $217,432 by one leading insurer for $1 million/$3 million of malpractice coverage,[24] amounts which were probably insufficient to protect him.

Some of the causes of expansion are the same in this field as in product liability: the reliance on juries to decide intricate technical questions and to calculate damages, the payment of claimants' lawyers by contingency fees, and the use of partisan expert witnesses. Some are unique to this field: the high injury rates associated with modern medical treatment, the extremely high costs of long-term medical treatment, the extremely long periods of liability (21 years for injuries incurred during birth) and the availability of multiple, affluent defendants in most cases, since hospitals can be sued for whatever doctors do within their walls.

But the most striking feature of the medical malpractice system is its failure to compensate the vast majority of legitimate claimants, that is, of patients negligently injured in the course of medical treatment. The Harvard study of patients admitted to a large sample of hospitals in New York State in 1984 found that about 1 percent of them were negligently injured in the course of hospitalization but fewer than 1 in 60 of these people received any compensation for their injury. Three times as many patients were injured nonnegligently and *none* of them were compensated.[25]

There are very few existing arrangements to enable health care providers to compensate injured patients voluntarily. The fear of stimulating a malpractice suit, with unpredictable consequences, ordinarily makes an offer of voluntary compensation unthinkable.

But the tort remedy is only available to patients with large claims—for wrongful death, permanent paralysis, severe disfigurement and the like. It is a matter of simple arithmetic. As one plaintiff's attorney explained to me, it costs him about $35,000 to prepare and conduct a malpractice case, which he has about a 50 percent chance of winning, and which, if he does win, will pay him 35 percent of the award, so that it is imprudent for him to take on a case that does not offer the possibility of an award over $200,000. But most medical injuries are not worth nearly that much, and so the sufferers have no recourse at all.[26]

The Harvard study estimated that $894 million would have been enough to pay for the medical expenses and lost income of all the patients in New York State who were injured, *with or without negligence*, during hospitalization in the study year. That amount would have been somewhat less than physicians and hospitals actually paid that year for the malpractice insurance that compensated only a tiny fraction of the victims.[27]

The anxiety of physicians concerning malpractice suits is not all bad, of course. Some of the general practitioners who have given up surgery for fear of being sued were not very good surgeons. Some of the extra tests that are ordered in the name of defensive medicine disclose problems that would otherwise be overlooked. Some of the innovative drugs that physicians hesitate to prescribe are later discovered to have severe side effects.

But the costs outweigh the benefits. The two major functions of malpractice liability are compensation and deterrence and, as we have just seen, the system's compensation performance is laughable. Its deterrence performance is hampered by the absence of experience rating in malpractice premiums and by another very interesting phenomenon—the reluctance of physicians to criticize or discipline incompetent colleagues for fear of incurring another type of liability. Physicians serving on official peer review panels have indeed been successfully sued for damaging the professional reputations of those whom they judged to be incompetent.[28]

There are no real limits to this game. In one neat turnaround, a Maryland law firm was sued for legal malpractice by a plaintiff who accused them of mishandling her suit for medical malpractice. A jury awarded her the amount she had claimed in her medical malpractice suit.[29] The relatively new fields of legal, accounting and engineering malpractice have been growing by leaps and bounds.

The need for reform in the medical sector of the liability system is obvious. In 1975, during one of the malpractice crises that occur every few years, 20 states passed laws involving one or more reforms: shortening the statute of limitations, limiting the size of contingency fees, eliminating the collateral source rule that permits recovering the same damages from more than one source, redefining terms such as "informed consent" and "standard of care." Twenty-one states passed laws imposing new requirements on insurance carriers. Twelve states passed laws expanding the powers of state medical disciplinary boards. The health care professionals lobbied against the lawyers and the insurance companies who were causing them pain. In 1987, in response to a later malpractice crisis, 22 states passed reform legislation dealing with medical liability. These were a little more sophisticated and included such things as caps on awards for pain and suffering, and minimum qualifications for expert witnesses. A cap on pain and suffering awards is also included in currently proposed federal legislation. A few states have established pretrial screening procedures, which have the unintended effect of adding to the cost and delay of litigation. Two states, Virginia and Florida, have enacted no-fault compensation for a single category of claimants: brain-damaged infants.[30]

This torrent of reform legislation did not significantly change the status quo in medical liability and many of the new enactments were declared unconstitutional when challenged in state courts. In the war between doctors and lawyers, legislatures have half-heart-edly sided with the doctors but the courts have stayed loyal to their own, resisting most of the efforts to cure the defects of the adversarial system in this area.

The settlement of malpractice claims by means of binding arbitration has been tried here and there with some success. In one experimental format,[31] claimants and defendants, represented by counsel, agreed to submit a case to arbitration and to accept the decision of the arbitrators without the possibility of appeal. Both sides submitted their evidence in writing, the arbitration service consulted experts of its own choosing to resolve medical and legal issues, and the case was then heard by a three-member panel composed of a physician, a plaintiffs' lawyer and a knowledgeable layman. If the panel found the claim to be valid, it determined the amount of compensation and notified the parties. The cost and delay were trivial compared to litigation. The arbitration service charged a flat fee of $2,500 per case and settled every case within 60 days after the parties completed their filings. This procedure avoided the worst features of ordinary malpractice litigation and could deal with small claims as well as large ones. The experimental service successfully handled all of the cases brought to it, but did not muster the necessary support from the plaintiffs' bar, which perceived it as a threat.

LANDOWNERS' AND MUNICIPAL LIABILITY

The liability of landowners for injuries that occur on their property and the broader liability of municipal agencies for injuries connected with public services have long been established in the common law, but until recently, claimants had to prove that their injuries had been caused by the negligence of the party from whom they claimed damages. In this sector as in others, the rules of the legal game have changed dramatically in the past two decades. But unlike product liability, where moral responsibility has dropped out of the picture by removing the requirement of negligence, the expansion of landowner and municipal liability has been accomplished by enlarging the concept of negligence to include the failure of a landlord or municipality to anticipate and prevent criminal and irresponsible actions by other parties, including claimants.

Thus, it has become routine for women raped in or near their apartments to sue the landlord for not having installed more lighting in the parking lot or better locks on the front door. In 1991, a Texas jury awarded a woman $14 million from the owners of her townhouse complex because a rapist stole her address and key from the office.[32]

In 1992, the U.S. Supreme Court authorized a former Georgia high school student who alleged sexual harassment by a teacher to sue the local school board for damages,[33] and went on to announce the applicability of this new rule to all schools receiving federal funds.

The actions of the complainant, however irresponsible, no longer weigh in the balance. A Washington, D.C., woman was rinsing her baby daughter in a bathroom sink and left her alone there while she went to attend to a child in another room. Another little child came in to the bathroom, turned on the hot water and scalded the baby severely. The case against the building's owners and managers, and some associated defendants, was settled during trial for the tidy sum of $15 million.[34]

It has become routine for municipalities to be held liable for drownings in park lakes, runaway horses in parades and similar incidents over which they have no effective control. Even an ordinance that prohibits swimming in the lake and a posted warning are unlikely to protect the town against suit if someone sneaks in and contrives to drown. Liability insurance has become one of the major costs of local government, but it is often unaffordable and sometimes unobtainable. A few municipalities have ceased to function altogether in the face of this problem. And almost every local government or public agency in the United States has curtailed or abandoned worthwhile activities for fear of being sued. No other country in the world inflicts problems like this on its local officials. The costs, of course, are passed on to the public.

WORKERS' COMPENSATION

Workers' compensation, the next field of liability to be considered, is organized quite differently. Throughout the United States, employers are liable for work-related injuries suffered by their employees, even if caused by the negligence of the injured worker or by fellow workers. The employer's liability is limited to the payment of medical expenses and the replacement of lost wages. Most jurisdictions require employers to carry workers' compensation insurance to cover this risk. The insurance is available at reasonable rates.

The first workers' compensation plan was introduced in Germany in 1884. It began to be imitated at once. By 1900, 11 nations had such programs; by 1987, at least 136 nations had them. In most of them, workers' compensation was the first social insurance program to be adopted.[35] That was true of the United States, which began with the Federal Employers Liability Act, enacted by Congress in 1908 to compensate railroad employees injured or killed on the job (there were 12,000 deaths in the railroad industry that year, compared to 48 in 1988). That act, still in force, did not establish a no-fault system; the employee had to prove negligence on the part of the employer. But soon afterwards, the states began to establish workers' compensation programs with the two essential features that identify the type: they are no-fault and they compensate only economic losses.[36]

Until the 1970s, most of these plans were underfunded so that the benefits received by injured workers did not fully replace their lost wages. That has recently been corrected, and benefit levels are now close to what experts consider to be the appropriate level.[37]

By and large, it works well. The overhead costs are much lower than in other liability fields, the coverage of injuries much more inclusive, the delays and uncertainties much less, the allocation of risk more reasonable. But this branch of the liability tree is not totally immune from the blight in other branches.

The liability revolution threatens the stability of workers' compensation in several different ways. In recent years, courts have permitted injured workers, although fully covered by workers' compensation, to sue third parties, especially the manufacturers of workplace machines and equipment, for personal injury damages based on alleged defects of design and warning. Some courts have also permitted "dual capacity" suits against an employer, for example, in the employer's capacity of installer of workplace equipment. These innovations undermine the successful bargain embodied in workers' compensation, whereby the employers assume liability for workplace injuries without regard to negligence in return for the workers' acceptance of predictable compensation. Finally, in California and some other states where legal ingenuity is especially unrestrained, workers' compensation programs have recently been required to pay claims for invisible injuries, notably stress. In those jurisdictions, a worker worried about being laid off can now allege that he was disabled thereby. Invisible injuries can not be proved or disproved. In jurisdictions that admit this category of claims, they are likely to wreck workers' compensation beyond repair.

Compensation for occupational diseases presents many more problems than compensation for injuries on the job. Workers' compensation programs are not well equipped to deal with disease claims. Typically, such diseases show up many years after exposure to workplace hazards and their causation is often uncertain. The most important episode of litigation concerning occupational diseases followed the discovery that mesothelioma and asbestositis are caused by sustained exposure to asbestos. Thousands of lawsuits by former asbestos workers were presented and settled; the companies producing asbestos and asbestos products went into bankruptcy, yet it is known that many valid claims were never presented. In Canada where asbestos claims were processed under workers' compensation, the results seem to have been more equitable and the economic impact less severe.[38] One reason was that medical expense was not a factor in Canada, which has universal health insurance. Another was that the legal expenses were enormous in the United States and negligible in Canada.

The compensation of coal miners' black lung disease, undertaken since 1970 by the federal government, has been complicated by the fact that black lung disease cannot be clinically distinguished from other forms of pulmonary impairment, such as those associated with cigarette smoking. The eventual number of claims far exceeded the original estimates, and the program was eventually expanded to cover coal miners or former miners with any respiratory impairment. The cost is financed by a special tax on coal.[39]

Neither workers' compensation nor litigation are very effective in coping with occupational disease. Disability allowances from Social Security and private insurance are more efficient in replacing lost wages; health insurance is a better way of paying medical expenses; regulation appears to be more effective in promoting workplace safety.

AUTOMOTIVE LIABILITY

Measured by the volume of litigation, automotive liability is the largest field of the liability system. It accounts for about half of the total number of liability suits in state courts. Like the other fields, it has been extensively redesigned since 1965; by the adoption of no-fault legislation in 24 states, by a shift from contributory to comparative negligence in 33 states and by mandatory insurance requirements in all states.

No-fault statutes take some of the claims arising from automobile accidents out of the courts by making drivers and owners of vehicles, and of course their insurers, responsible for the damages they cause without reference to fault. But none of the no-fault statutes limits the right to sue on a claim of death or serious injury;[40] the cases removed from the courts involve only collision damage and minor injuries, and the pocketbooks of trial lawyers are hardly affected at all.

As of 1989, only five states still applied the common law rule of contributory negligence to automobile cases (the rule which made it impossible, for example, for a jaywalking pedestrian struck by a drunken driver to be compensated). All the other states permit recovery when there is some degree of negligence on the part of the victim. The precise degree, stated as a percentage estimate, varies from state to state, and in many states, an award is reduced by that same proportion—another scientifically challenging calculation that juries are called on to perform.

Mandatory liability insurance for vehicle owners makes obvious good sense. But the relationship between the insurance companies and their customers is not a very happy one. Fraud in the pricing of insurance claims is widespread. In thousands of body shops across the country, an "insurance job" costs more than an ordinary job, can include repairs unrelated to the accident, and may involve a cash rebate to the customer. Some doctors operate in the same way, providing a diagnosis of whiplash on demand and billing for patient visits that never occur.[41]

The insurance companies do not behave impeccably either. They skim the market by refusing to insure drivers they consider high risk, who must then in one way or another be insured by the state. They commonly set premiums according to irrelevant criteria, refuse coverage to people who live in redlined areas, cancel the policies of customers who submit claims, raise premiums excessively after minor traffic violations, refuse customers whose insurance has been canceled by competitors, collude with competitors on prices, withdraw from states that try to improve regulation, and take general advantage of their situation as sellers of an essential service which they are not compelled to make available.[42]

Moreover, every state has a great number of uninsured drivers, who are likely to be poor drivers in both senses, and when they cause accidents, their victims may have no recourse at all, although a few states provide limited compensation from a public fund.

With respect to property damage, automotive liability operates more smoothly than the other sectors of the liability system. The question of liability is commonly resolved at the time of the accident, if one or more drivers are ticketed for moving violations. The great majority of claims are settled between insurers, without the intervention of amateurs.

With respect to personal injuries, automotive liability is much less efficient and much more costly. According to one critic,

Approximately a third of the premium dollar goes to insurance companies and agents for selling and administering the policies and for profit. Nearly a quarter goes to lawyers and claims investigators for wrangling over who was at fault. Nearly a dime goes for the reimbursement of medical costs already reimbursed by other insurance plans. Twenty odd cents goes to pay for pain and suffering which, in all too many cases means overpayments on small or meritless claims, just to get them off the books. And finally, about 15 cents goes to pay for actual non-reimbursed medical expenses and lost wages.[43]

Another critic describes the courts in the 1970s as overwhelmed, swamped and choked by the futile effort to decide who hit whom on the highway in thousands and thousands of cases.[44] But this inexpensive and inequitable system is relatively stable. It does not show the cancerous growth that afflicts the other branches of the liability system.

In automotive cases, juries are more restrained than in product liability or malpractice cases. Their judgments, based on personal experience, are better informed and their awards seem to be proportioned to their own insurance coverages. Where the jury in a product liability case might bring in a verdict of $10 million for the death of an infant, a jury's assessment of the same loss in an automotive case might be 1 or 2 percent of that amount. Additionally, there is the happy circumstance that automotive liability cases are rather uninteresting from a legal standpoint and thus do not tempt judges to make new law.

THE SEARCH FOR SOLUTIONS

Designing a viable reform of the more irrational branches of the liability system—product liability, environmental liability, malpractice liability, landowners' and municipal liability—is a mind-boggling task, given the complexity of the issues and the number of players. Any serious reform must modify the legal structure which has been built piece by piece by Congress and 50 state legislatures, and by hundreds of appellate courts. Standing squarely in the way of the most obvious reform, which would do away with juries in liability cases, is the formidable obstacle of the Seventh Amendment to the U.S. Constitution: "In suits at common law, where the value in controversy shall exceed twenty dollars, the right of trial by jury shall be preserved, and no fact tried by a jury shall be otherwise re-examined in any Court of the United States, than according to the rules of the common law." So there is no hope of removing juries from the adversarial processing of liability claims.

Nevertheless, something must be done. The liability system in its present form is intolerable. Aside from imposing a competitive handicap on American enterprises, it hobbles all sorts of useful activities, such as engineering and sports, without accomplishing anything that could not be better done by using production standards to minimize product defects, legislation to maintain environmental quality, patients' compensation to cover medical injuries, first-party insurance to cover traffic injuries, universal health insurance to take care of medical expenses and disciplinary measures—including criminal prosecution—to deter serious negligence in any field.

Because the liability system is so diverse, its defects must be repaired piecemeal. The only potential remedy that cuts across the board is the recommendation of the Committee for Economic Development that statutory schedules should be established for determining compensation for monetary and nonmonetary losses in personal injury cases, so that juries would have firm guidelines for assessing damages, taking into account the age, earning power and other relevant characteristics of the plaintiff. Monetary losses would ordinarily cover lost earnings and medical expenses. Persons without earning power, such as children and retired people, would receive a sum equivalent to the average allowance for lost earnings. Such schedules would of course be indexed for inflation. Nonmonetary losses, primarily for pain and suffering, would be limited to specified conditions, such as paralysis, and would be calculated as a fixed percentage of monetary losses.[45]

Another statutory reform that appears to be constitutional would be the setting of minimum thresholds for defendants' liability, so that, for example, a defendant whose contribution to a harm was less than 25 percent could not be held liable. That would not free juries from having to make implausible calculations, but it would shift the burden of proof from defendants to plaintiffs, where that burden properly belongs.

In product liability, the most urgent need is legislation that immunizes producers from liability if they comply with government specifications about product design and warning notices. It may be too late to rescue the general aviation industry but that would be a good place to start, since the design and testing of light planes is already fully regulated and the adequacy of those controls is suggested by the fact that, unlike juries, expert investigators do not attribute light aircraft accidents to faulty design or information. In the drug industry, the FDA review of new products before they are marketed is thoroughgoing and meticulous. That does not preclude the later appearance of unsuspected side effects in new products, but the social cost of penalizing pharmaceutical innovation outweighs the benefits. Other products that particularly invite litigation—ladders, machine tools, children's toys—should be reviewed and regulated in the same way, and compliance with the regulations should be a complete defense against liability claims.

Environmental liability comes the closest of anything described in this book to be unreformable. The core problem is the gullibility of juries when they are called on to resolve difficult questions of causation. But the constitutional right to a jury trial is irremovable. The establishment of compensation schedules, and of contribution thresholds, would be helpful here, and so would the abolition of contingency fees in class action suits. Requiring the expenses of such a suit to be raised by voluntary contributions from the plaintiffs would not deprive the poor of access to the courts—the customary rationale for contingency fees—since the plaintiffs in class action suits are so numerous that small contributions from them would add up to large fees for their lawyers. But without giant windfalls, the incentives for law firms to organize environmental suits would be much reduced.

In the medical malpractice sector, as we saw, there are not only the usual tort liability problems of delay, uncertainty, inequity and very high overhead costs, but also the special and urgent problem that the overwhelming majority of medical injuries are not compensated at all. These problems can be addressed together by imitating the generally successful experience of workers' compensation. Under a patients' compensation scheme, patients injured in the course of medical treatment, by negligence or otherwise, would be able to recover their lost earnings and their medical expenses from the responsible provider, whose liability would be covered and limited by the patients' compensation insurance that all providers would be required to carry. Persons outside the labor force would be compensated at a rate equivalent to the average earnings of employed persons. Cases of disputed causation would be resolved by an arbitration panel, composed equally of provider and patient representatives, which would investigate the facts independently and consult experts of its own choosing.

Patients' compensation insurance would be experience-rated, and providers with exceptionally poor experience would be automatically referred to professional review boards for possible disciplinary action.

Patients' compensation could be established by statute and made obligatory for all health care providers in a jurisdiction. But it might also be established by contract between individual providers and their patients, stipulating the providers' assumption of no-fault liability, the schedule of compensation payments and the agreement of the parties to submit disputes about causation to compulsory arbitration. These private arrangements would require statutory authorization, exempting those providers who elected patients' compensation from malpractice liability. It would require local coordination, since physicians and other providers offering patients' compensation would need access to a hospital with the same arrangement.

Such legislation would undoubtedly be challenged in court, since it poses a threat to the economic interests of the plaintiffs' bar, but given the strong precedent of workers' compensation, it would likely survive the challenge.

In landowners' and municipal liability, the most serious problem is the overpricing of insurance. This could probably be cured by statutory scheduling of compensation and a threshold to immunize defendants whose contribution to the harm was minimal.

Workers' compensation works better than any other part of the liability system in compensating injuries on the job. Because insurance premiums are steeply graded by loss experience, they provide a strong incentive for employers to reduce workplace hazards. The overhead costs are extremely low compared to the other branches of the liability system.

Workers' compensation is very effective in dealing with ordinary workplace injuries. It is not effective with respect to occupational diseases, which typically appear after a lapse of many years and whose causation is almost always disputable. This category of claims really belongs to the environmental liability branch of the liability system and shares the intractable problems of that type of liability. Scheduled compensation, a minimum threshold of contribution to harm and the abolition of contingency fees in class action suits is what might be done to palliate the excesses of environmental liability. A better solution would be to shift the burden of compensation for all environmental injuries, including occupa-

tional diseases, out of the liability system altogether, to universal
health insurance and to government disability programs.

The problems of automotive liability, as previously noted, are
serious but not desperate. Scheduled compensation and the prohibition of dual recovery for medical expenses would help. So would
stricter state regulation of the insurance industry. But the need for
reform is more urgent in the other branches of the liability system.

NOTES

1. George L. Priest, "The Modern Expansion of Tort Liability: Its
Sources, Its Effects and Its Reform," *Journal of Economic Perspectives* 5,
no. 3, (1991): 38.

2. See, among other sources, Gary T. Schwartz, "Product Liability
and Medical Malpractice in Comparative Perspective," in *The Liability
Maze: The Impact of Liability Law on Safety and Innovation*, edited by Peter
W. Huber and Robert E. Litan (Washington, DC: The Brookings Institu-
tion, 1991); Office of Economic Development, *Automobile Insurance and
Road Accident Prevention* (Paris: OECD Publication Service, 1990).

3. There are severe current problems in some of the excluded fields,
including directors' and officers' liability, educational liability, nonmedi-
cal malpractice and the brand-new field of sexual abuse liability, but
space does not allow them to be considered here.

4. Robert Martin, "General Aviation Manufacturing: An Industry
Under Siege," and Andrew Craig, "Product Liability and Safety in General Aviation," in Huber and Litan, *The Liability Maze*.

5. "In 1986, at the request of a Congressional committee, Beech
analyzed the 203 accidents involving its planes between 1983 and 1986.
Each was investigated by the NTSB and/or the FAA. 118 were attributed
to pilot error, 23 to maintenance, 21 to weather, 63 to unknown causes,
none to aircraft design. But the average amount claimed per accident was
$10 million, and average cost to Beech of each accident was $530,000."
Martin, "General Aviation Manufacturing," 485-486.

6. Huber has traced the history of litigation against Benedictin, an
antinauseant drug formerly prescribed for pregnant women. A flock of
lawsuits, some successful, alleged that the product caused birth defects,
despite overwhelming clinical evidence to the contrary. The drug was
eventually withdrawn to reduce the costs of litigation. No products of
this type remain on the market or are likely to be introduced. Peter
Huber, *Galileo's Revenge: Junk Science in the Courtroom* (New York: Basic
Books, 1991).

7. And even to transplanted foreign companies, like the American subsidiaries of Honda and Volkswagen, who do not suffer from the vast potential liabilities attached to vehicles produced and sold long ago.

8. Warren Brown, "GM Found Negligent in Fuel Tank Case," *Washington Post* (February 5, 1993): A1, A4; Howard Kurtz, "NBC Apologizes for Staged Crash, Settles with GM," *Washington Post* (February 10, 1993): A1, A15.

9. In March 1991, the U.S. Supreme Court, in *Pacific Mutual Liability Co. v. Haslip* ruled that punitive damages far in excess of actual losses did not violate due process "so long as juries' discretion is exercised within reasonable constraints." Punitive damages in that case were $840,000 against a loss of $3,800. The Court did not define "reasonable constraints." Carl Shapiro, "Symposium on the Economics of Liability," *Journal of Economic Perspectives* 5, no. 3 (1991): 3–10.

10. *Beshada v. Johns-Manville*, New Jersey, 1962.

11. *Moran v. Faberge, Inc.*, Maryland, 1975.

12. *Rogers v. Toro Manufacturing Company*, Misssouri, 1975.

13. *Ferebee v. Chevron Chemical Company*, DC Federal District Court, 1984.

14. Walter Olson, "Overdeterrence and the Problem of Comparative Risk," *Proceedings of the Academy of Political Science* 37, no. 1 (1988): 44–45.

15. George L. Priest, "Understanding the Liability Crisis," *Proceedings of the Academy of Political Science* 37, no. 1 (1988): 196–211; see also *Statistical Abstract of the United States 1992*, Tables 113, 114, 123, 184, 665, 1177.

16. These are detailed in U.S. Congress, Joint Economic Committee, *The Cost of the Tort System*, 99th Cong., 2d sess., S. Hrg. 99–1090 (1986).

17. Bruce Yandle, "Rules of Liability and the Demise of Superfund," in *The Economic Consequences of Liability Rules: In Defense of Common Law Liability*, edited by Roger E. Meiners and Bruce Yandle (New York: Quorum Books, 1991). No adverse health effects from the Love Canal pollution were ever discovered but the impression that the health of residents was severely affected persists to this day.

18. The Comprehensive Environmental Response, Compensation and Recovery Act, 1980.

19. Peter Huber, "Environmental Hazards and Liability Law," in *Liability: Perspectives and Policy*, edited by Robert E. Litan and Clifford Winston (Washington, DC: The Brookings Institution, 1988), 136.

20. Ibid., 145.

21. Patricia M. Danzon, *Medical Malpractice: Theory, Evidence and Public Policy* (Cambridge, MA: Harvard University Press, 1985); "Liability for Medical Malpractice," *Journal of Economic Perspectives* 5, no. 3 (1991): 51–69.

22. V.P. Rostow, M. Osterweis and R. J. Bulger, "Medical Malpractice and the Delivery of Obstetrical Care," *New England Journal of Medicine* 321, no. 15 (October 1989): 1057–1060; Virginia Health Planning Board, *Access to Obstetrical Care*, Senate Document No. 27 (Richmond, VA: 1990).

23. Stanley Joel Reiser, "Malpractice, Patient Safety, and the Ethical and Scientific Foundations of Medicine," in Huber and Litan, *The Liability Maze*.

24. St. Paul's Fire and Casualty, *Physicians' and Surgeons Update: The St. Paul's 1989 Annual Report to Shareholders*, no. 9422, ed. 5–89 (St. Paul, MN: The St. Paul Companies, Medical Services Division, 1989).

25. Harvard Medical Practice Study, *Patients, Doctors, Lawyers: Medical Injury, Malpractice Litigation, and Patient Compensation* (Cambridge, MA: President and Fellows of Harvard College, 1990).

26. For additional discussion of this point, see U.S. General Accounting Office, *Medical Malpractice: A Framework for Action*, GAO/HRD-87–73 (Washington, DC: GAO, 1987).

27. Harvard Medical Practice Study, *Patients, Doctors, Lawyers*.

28. A federal law, the Health Care Quality Improvement Act of 1986, provided peer group reviewers with limited immunity for liability, but did not calm the apprehension of physicians. The same act established a national data bank to record disciplinary actions against physicians and verdicts and settlements in malpractice claims. As of 1994, it is not yet fully operative.

29. I am unable to locate a citation for this case but had first-hand knowledge of it at the time.

30. American College of Surgeons, "Medical Professional Liability: State Legislative Attempts at Reform," *Issues and Perspectives* (August 1989): 1–4.

31. The University of Virginia's Medical Mediation Service, directed by the author from 1989 to 1991.

32. Associated Press, "Rape Victim Wins $14 Million Award," *Charlottesville Daily Progress* (May 18, 1991): A2.

33. *Franklin v. Gwinnett County Public Schools*, February 1992.

34. Michael York, "Child Scalded in Sink Awarded $15 Million," *Washington Post*, May 27, 1992: D1, D2.

35. C. Arthur Williams, Jr., *An International Comparison of Workers' Compensation* (Boston: Kluwer Academic Publishers, 1991).

36. This history is nicely summarized in U.S. Congress, House, Committee on Energy and Commerce, *Federal Employers' Liability Act*, Serial No. 101–109 (1989).

37. Arthur Larson, "Tensions of the Next Decade," in *New Perspectives in Workers' Compensation*, edited by John F. Burton, Jr. (Ithaca, NY: H.R. Press, 1988), 21–44.

38. Donald M. Dewees, "Paying for Asbestos-Related Diseases Under Workers' Compensation," in Burton, *New Perspectives*; Michael J. Moore and W. Kip Viscusi, *Compensation Mechanisms for Job Risks: Wages, Workers' Compensation, and Product Liability* (Princeton, NJ: Princeton University Press, 1990).

39. Peter S. Barth, *The Tragedy of Black Lung: Federal Compensation for Occupational Disease* (Kalamazoo, MI: W. E. Upjohn Institute for Employment Research, 1987).

40. Joseph E. Johnson, George B. Flanigan and Daniel T. Winkler, "Cost Implications of No-Fault Automobile Insurance," *Journal of Risk and Insurance* 59, no. 1 (1992): 116–223.

41. U.S. Congress, House, Committee on Energy and Commerce, *Automobile Insurance*, Series No. 101–13 (1989).

42. U.S. Congress, House, Committee on Energy and Commerce, *Automobile Insurance*, Serial No. 100–151 (1988).

43. Ibid., testimony of Andrew Tobias before the committee, 4.

44. Ibid., quoting Daniel Patrick Moynihan, 5.

45. Committee for Economic Development, *Who Should be Liable: A Guide to Policy for Dealing with Risk* (New York: Committee for Economic Development, 1989), 133–134.

8

WHAT SHOULD BE DONE?

Most of the problems of our five failing systems revolve around money. In the health care system, the pricing of goods and services is irrational and unfair. In the education system, the problems connected with money are more subtle but equally real: the inability to get more productivity by spending more money and the inequities in school spending among localities. The essential problem of the welfare system is that its clients get less money than they need for a comfortable life but more than other people think they deserve. The dominating problem of the criminal justice system is that the futile effort to prohibit certain euphoriant drugs has increased the cost and complexity of law enforcement, and has directed a vast stream of money to drug traffickers. The liability system take large sums of money from the productive parts of the national economy and wastes them on its own clumsy procedures. Somehow, we seem to have lost the knack of allocating money wisely to collective purposes.

When new money is injected into a social system without careful safeguards, the more powerful actors in that system will take the lion's share of it and ask for more. That is what happened in these cases. In the health care system, money intended to improve the quality and availability of care was misdirected to raising the incomes of providers and the profits of suppliers. In the education system, the new money went to reduce class size and raise teachers' salaries, but did nothing to increase productivity. In the welfare system, money has been effectively used to improve the earnings and career prospects of officials, but not to help people extricate themselves from poverty. In the justice system, large sums of money have been diverted into drug enforcement, without any social benefit. The liability system gives huge monetary rewards to lawyers and insurance companies, while imposing heavy burdens on the rest of us.

These monetary abuses tend to perpetuate themselves. The great infusion of public money into the health care system inflated the income of physicians beyond all reason, thereby giving them the incentive and the resources to lobby effectively against any effective limitation of medical costs. The successful salary-raising efforts of the teachers' unions have earned them the loyalty of their members and the funds to fight any project of educational improvement that does not involve budgetary expansion. The social workers who run the welfare system look less intimidating than the professionals in other fields but they are just as well entrenched, so that every change in welfare policy seems to entail increased administration. Most of the huge war chest of the war on drugs is spent on law enforcement professionals, whose enlarged influence is vigorously deployed to defend their new privileges. In the liability system, the rich and ingenious lawyers of the plaintiffs' bar are admirably situated to block efforts at reform.

The professionals did not create the perverse incentives in these systems but they are now attached to them by the strong bond of monetary self-interest. Nearly everyone involved in the five failing systems knows that reforms are needed. But it is taken for granted by knowledgeable observers that the resistance of professional interest groups make fundamental changes unlikely until the defects of a system drive it to a point just short of catastrophe.

The health care system arrived at that point in the early 1990s. Not everyone would agree that the education or welfare systems are there yet but they are generally conceded to be close. The criminal justice system may be considered to have passed from imminent to actual catastrophe but public opinion will not yet support the changes that are plainly called for. In the liability system, the catastrophe is compartmented and partly hidden from public view.

Nowhere in the political spectrum is there a faction that defends the pricing of health insurance, the productivity of the schools, the fairness of welfare or the efficiency of crime control. There is a national consensus that something must be done about education, that the welfare system is a disgrace, that prisons are dangerously overcrowded, that the burden of liability insurance is ruinous. But, except in the case of health care, the search for solutions has been slow and uninspired.

The accepted strategy of reformers in contemporary American society is to wait until the problems they want to solve become severe enough to generate wide support for change. The drawback of this approach is that by the time public opinion builds to the necessary level, the problems may be intractable. But it cannot be denied that as the sense of crisis deepens, reforms which were once unthinkable move into the domain of practical action. Ten years ago the health care system was almost impervious to criticism; today, a national consensus is pushing it into unfamiliar territory. Something similar will eventually overtake our zany drug policies, the primitive teaching methods of the public schools and the doctrine of environmental liability.

Regrettably, we cannot be sure that when the propitious moment arrives, effective reforms will prevail over futile ones. They are not always easy to tell apart. Effective reform projects respect the basic principles of social technology. They identify core problems and root causes, specify precise objectives, accept incurred costs, monitor results, provide for continuous attention to incentives, and anticipate midcourse corrections. Futile reform projects are designed to create the illusion of change without excessively disturbing the status quo: diagnostic related groups (DRGs), workfare, competency testing, mandatory sentences and limited no-fault laws illustrate in various ways how this can be done. DRGs do not remove the incentives of health care providers to raise their prices continuously. Workfare does not change the incentives of welfare clients to avoid marriage; it creates new incentives to avoid employment. Competency testing does not remove the incentives of teachers to limit their output. Mandatory sentences enhance the perverse incentives that sustain the illegal drug market. Limited no-fault laws do not touch the profits of the plaintiffs' bar.

In the foregoing chapters, I have tried to identify some of the measures that might actually reduce or remove the perverse incentives that now dominate these systems. In health care, the limitation of aggregate expenditures to a fixed percentage of GDP, or of payrolls, appears to be essential. Other reforms would follow of themselves if that one were in place.

In the public schools, the basic problem is low productivity. A higher level of funding would not solve that problem. We already spend more on public education than other countries and get less for it. A significant increase of productivity can be achieved by introducing national tests at all grade levels, computerizing the classroom, enlarging the professional authority of teachers and equalizing per pupil expenditures among school districts. These reforms should produce enough real savings to hold school expenditures at a fixed proportion of state and local budgets, and raise teachers' salaries at the same time.

In the welfare system, the basic problem is the formation and persistence of poor, female-headed families. The most promising way of reducing the number of such families is to remove the marginal taxes that make it unprofitable for poor women to marry, take jobs or save. But this cannot be done in the existing system without allowing welfare clients to have higher incomes than those of the working poor. The only way out of the box is to abandon Aid to Families with Dependent Children altogether and substitute a universal family allowance.

The war on drugs has become the basic problem of the criminal justice system. As long as the government continues to operate its elaborate machinery for keeping drug prices high and guaranteeing extraordinary profits to drug traffickers, no significant reform is likely. The incarceration mania and the destruction of the social fabric that accompanies it will continue until the unhappy experiment of drug prohibition is terminated. But the adverse consequences of the incarceration mania can be alleviated in the meantime by substituting other forms of restraint for imprisonment.

With respect to liability, the basic problem is the adversarial method of processing injury claims in the law courts. The lawyers who operate that process have a perverse incentive to make the settlement of claims slow, complex and uncertain because every delay and uncertainty creates additional fees. There is nothing about the average injury claim that could not be better handled by an independent investigation of the facts and the determination of awards by an impartial panel according to a fixed schedule of payments. Most of the money paid into the system would then go to injured claimants and not as it does now, to lawyers and insurers.

There are, it appears, quite practicable remedies for the ills of the five failing systems. But are they politically feasible? The answer to this question has less to do with party politics than might be expected. Most physicians vote Republican most of the time. Teachers and social workers are more likely to identify themselves as Democrats. The agents of law enforcement are divided between the two major parties, as are lawyers. Republican legislators are traditionally responsive to medical lobbyists. Democrats are notably sympathetic to the teachers' unions. But the legislatures that pass tort reform measures under medical pressure are as likely to have Democratic as Republican majorities. The most serious effort to replace welfare payments by a form of family allowance was made by a Republican administration in 1971. Increases in educational funding often enjoy bipartisan backing. The escalation of the war on drugs is enthusiastically supported by both parties. The judges who continually expand the concept of liability owe their appointments to both parties. The defects in the five failing systems carry no party label and, with the exception of a tilt toward the medical profession and a little more animus toward welfare clients on the Republican side, the two major parties do not differ very much in their responsiveness to reform proposals.

It is not the political parties that stand in the way of effective reform, but the pressure groups that bring their influence to bear on the representatives elected by either party. An attempt at *gradual* reform in any of the five failing systems will almost surely be defeated by the resistance of the professionals who operate the system. They can contrive to transform reforms like cost containment or job training into reinforcements of the status quo, as has happened again and again in these systems during the past twenty years.

If gradual reform is impracticable, what are the alternatives? One option is drastic reform—a sudden, sweeping change in the rules of the game. Another is the creation of a parallel system to compete with the existing system.

The first option—drastic reform—is superficially the more attractive. Why should we not move overnight to a health care system of the single-payer type, with the government as the universal insurer and negotiated payments to providers? Why not give annual national examinations to the entire school population and evaluate teachers by the progress of their pupils? Why not abolish welfare and substitute a universal family allowance? Why not decriminalize drugs? And why not initiate compulsory no-fault insurance, with a fixed schedule of payments, for every type of personal injury?

Some of these steps may eventually be taken. There have been moments of national despair or excitement—in 1933 and 1968, for example—when drastic reforms suddenly became feasible and were adopted overnight. But such occasions are few and far between and the impetus in each episode is short-lived. Under normal political conditions, drastic reform is effectively blocked by the opposition of influential, well-organized groups whose interests are tied to the status quo: physicians, hospitals, teachers, welfare officials, drug enforcers, lawyers, insurers.

Nor should their objections to drastic reform be lightly dismissed. The principle that incurred costs must be accepted guarantees that the substitution of rational procedures for some of our crazier ones would not be painless. Health care costs, having been pumped up to their present levels by perverse incentives, would not abruptly subside when the incentives were changed. Thousands of veteran teachers never learned how to teach effectively; it is probably too late for them to do so now. The families that were broken by the welfare system, or that never formed because of the welfare system, will not reconstitute themselves if the disincentives are removed. The American drug epidemic may be largely the product of drug prohibition but it would not now disappear if the prohibition were removed. In the liability system, the overcompensation of a few lucky litigants has raised the standard for compensation so high that universal insurance coverage may now be unaffordable.

The alternative reform strategy is the creation of a parallel system, constructed on better principles, to prove that the defects of the existing system can be removed and that their removal makes the new system more effective and efficient than the old. To qualify as more effective, the parallel system must be able to provide better service to more people. To qualify as more efficient, it must do it at lower cost.

The division of responsibility for the health care, education, welfare, criminal justice and liability systems among the federal government, the 50 states and thousands of local jurisdictions can be blamed for many of the defects of those systems, but it does have an advantage when it comes to the development of parallel systems. States and localities have more scope to experiment in these fields than they would have if national policy were more coherent. At least two states have already established universal health insurance; a number of states and localities have reorganized their schools to emphasize and reward productivity; other states have experimented with guaranteed income plans, substitutes for incarceration, and no-fault insurance. Every such experiment, successful or not, provides useful guidance for subsequent reforms.

Some parallel systems have been in place for long enough to provide very good models. The experience of health maintenance organizations (HMOs) provides an informative contrast to conventional health care arrangements. The private schools—both parochial and secular—that educate about one in seven American children consistently achieve better educational results than the public schools at much lower cost. A number of public and private poverty programs—food stamps, food banks, energy assistance—operate without the usual problems associated with welfare. Controlled maintenance drug programs, although not problem-free, are clearly more effective and efficient than the repressive approaches to drug addiction. For the compensation of injuries, binding arbitration is demonstrably faster, cheaper and more equitable than litigation.

Public awareness often lags behind discoveries in social technology, so that innovative models that succeed are not imitated as widely as they should be. The advocates of the status quo are always eager to discredit the parallel system that works, and their arguments always have some merit. HMOs have not found it easy to contain costs. Private schools tend to attract the educationally ambitious children of intact families. Food stamps are often used to buy luxury foods. Methadone is not significantly less addictive than heroin. Binding arbitration, which allows no appeals, deprives claimants of the opportunity to have unfavorable decisions reviewed.

But even if the parallel system does not offer a complete solution to the problems of the dominant system, its experience illuminates those problems and its mere existence undermines the position of those who defend the status quo on the grounds that nothing better is possible.

In democratic societies, big systems are seldom reformed by fiat. Most reform measures are compromises reached after prolonged negotiations in which all the interested parties make themselves heard. When some of the interested parties are professional groups with large investments in the status quo, they are likely to be better organized, better financed and more persistent than their opponents.

That is why effective reform comes so slowly. The problems we have been examining will not be solved overnight. But they do have to be solved, because the future of American society is at risk. The solutions, when they are found, will not be clean and neat, and the discussions leading up to them will not be conducted in a spirit of pure inquiry.

It is therefore crucially important that as many people as possible acquire an analytical understanding of these superficially complex problems. I have tried to show that their complexity is indeed superficial and would yield to rational problem-solving. Futile reforms that reinforce perverse incentives, such as harsher penalties for drug traffickers, will continue to be proposed and adopted, but if more and more of us attend to the root causes of the problems in these five failing systems, good sense and the public interest may eventually prevail over sociological ignorance and private greed.

SELECTED BIBLIOGRAPHY

Abraham, Kenneth. "The Causes of the Insurance Crisis." *Proceedings of the Academy of Political Science* 37, no. 1 (1988): 55–66.

American College of Surgeons. "Medical Professional Liability: State Legislative Attempts at Reform." *Issues and Perspectives*. (August 1989): 1–4.

American Journal of Public Health. "The German Health Care System: What Can We Learn from It?" 81 no. 9 (1991): 1157.

Athens, Lonnie H. *The Creation of Dangerous, Violent Criminals.* London: Routledge, 1989.

Bendich, Albert M. "Privacy, Poverty, and the Constitution." *California Law Review* 54, no. 2 (1966): 407–442.

Ben-Yehuda, Nachman. *The Politics and Morality of Deviance: Moral Panics, Drug Abuse, Deviant Science and Reversed Stigmatization.* Albany, NY: State University of New York Press, 1990.

Bergthold, Linda. *Purchasing Power in Health: Business, the State and Health Care Politics.* New Brunswick, NJ: Rutgers University Press, 1990.

Bogdanich, Walt. *The Great White Lie: How America's Hospitals Betray our Trust and Endanger our Lives.* New York: Simon and Schuster, 1991.

Burke, Dolores. *Physicians in the Academic Marketplace.* Westport, CT: Greenwood Press, 1991.

Burton, John F., Jr. *New Perspectives in Workers' Compensation.* Ithaca, NY: H.R. Press, 1988.

Califano, Joseph. *America's Health Care Revolution: Who Lives? Who Dies? Who Pays?* New York: Random House, 1986.

Campbell, Anne. *The Girls in the Gang.* 2d ed. Cambridge, MA: Basil Blackwell, 1991.

Caplow, Theodore. *American Social Trends.* San Diego: Harcourt Brace Jovanovich, 1991.

Caplow, Theodore, Howard M. Bahr, John Modell and Bruce A. Chadwick. *Recent Social Trends in the United States 1960–1990.* Frankfurt am Main: Campus Verlag; Montreal: McGill-Queens University Press, 1991.

Chall, Jeanne S., Vicki A. Jacobs and Luke E. Baldwin. *The Reading Crisis: Why Poor Children Fall Behind.* Cambridge, MA: Harvard University Press, 1990.

Coddington, Dean C., David J. Keen, Keith D. Moore and Richard L. Clarke. *The Crisis in Health Care.* San Francisco: Jossey-Bass, 1990.

Cohen, Stanley. *Visions of Social Control: Crime, Punishment and Classification.* Cambridge: Polity Press, 1985.

Committee for Economic Development. *Who Should be Liable? A Guide to Policy for Dealing with Risk.* New York: Committee for Economic Development, 1989.

Consumer Reports. "The Manufactured Crisis." (August 1986): 544–549.

Cooter, Robert D. "Economic Theories of Legal Liability." *Journal of Economic Perspectives* 5, no. 3 (1991): 11–30.

Cooter, Robert, and Stephen D. Sugarman. "A Regulated Market in Unmatured Tort Claims: Tort Reform by Contract." *Proceedings of the Academy of Political Science* 37, no. 1 (1988): 174–185.

Craig, Andrew. "Product Liability and Safety in General Aviation." In *The Liability Maze: The Impact of Liability Law on Safety and Innovation,* edited by Peter W. Huber and Robert E. Litan, 456–477. Washington, DC: The Brookings Institution, 1991.

Crispell, Kenneth R., and Carlos P. Gomez. "Proper Care for the Dying: A Critical Public Issue." *Journal of Medical Ethics* 13 (1987): 74–80.

Crozier, Michel. *Le Mal Americain.* Paris: Fayard, 1980.

Danzon, Patricia M. *Medical Malpractice: Theory, Evidence and Public Policy.* Cambridge, MA: Harvard University Press, 1985.

———. "Medical Malpractice Liability." In *Liability: Perspectives and Policy,* edited by Robert E. Litan and Clifford Winston, 101–127. Washington, DC: The Brookings Institution, 1988.

———. "Liability for Medical Malpractice." *Journal of Economic Perspectives* 5, no. 3 (Summer 1991): 51–69.

Davis, Kathy. *Power Under the Microscope.* Dordrecht, Holland: Foris Publications, 1988.

Dewees, Donald M. "Paying for Asbestos-Related Diseases Under Workers' Compensation." In *New Perspectives in Workers' Compensation*, edited by John F. Burton, Jr., 45–70. Ithaca, NY: H. R. Press, 1988.

Dionne, E. J., Jr. *Why Americans Hate Politics*. New York: Simon and Schuster, 1991.

Dirn, Louis. *La Société Française en Tendances*. Paris: Presses Universitaires de France, 1990.

Ehrenhalt, Alan. *United States of Ambition: Politicians, Power and the Pursuit of Office*. New York: Times Books, 1991.

Ellwood, David T. *Poor Support: Poverty in the American Family*. New York: Basic Books, 1988.

Elman, Richard M. *The Poorhouse State: The American Way of Life on Public Assistance*. New York: Random House, 1966.

Esping-Andersen, Gosta. *The Three Worlds of Welfare Capitalism*. Princeton, NJ: Princeton University Press, 1990.

Flanigan, George B., Joseph E. Johnson, Daniel T. Winkler and William Ferguson. "Experience from Early Tort Reforms: Comparative Negligence Since 1974." *Journal of Risk and Insurance* 56, no. 3 (1989): 525–534.

Fost, Norman, and Ronald E. Cranford. "Hospital Ethics Committees: Administrative Aspects." *Journal of the American Medical Association* 253, no. 18 (1985): 2687–2699.

Gilmore, Jeffrey L. *Price and Quality in Higher Education*. Washington, DC: Office of Educational Research and Improvement, Department of Education, 1990.

Glasgow, Douglas G. *The Black Underclass: Poverty, Unemployment and Entrapment of Ghetto Youth*. San Francisco: Jossey-Bass, 1980.

Goodwin, Leonard. *Causes and Cures of Welfare: New Evidence on the Social Psychology of the Poor*. Lexington, MA: Lexington Books, 1984.

Gottfredsom, Michael R., and Travis Hirschi. *A General Theory of Crime*. Stanford, CA: Stanford University Press, 1990.

Graham, John D., and Robert W. Crandall. "The Effect of Fuel Economy Standards on Automobile Safety." *Journal of Law and Economics* 32 (April 1989): 97–118.

Greenleaf, Sidney. *Impact*. New York: Bantam Books, 1989.

Handler, Joel F. *Reforming the Poor: Welfare Policy, Federalism and Morality*. New York: Basic Books, 1972.

Hans, Valerie P., and Neil Vidmar. *Judging the Jury*. New York: Plenum Press, 1986.

Harpham, Edward J., and Richard K. Scotch. "Rethinking the War on Poverty: The Ideology of Social Welfare Reform." *Western Political Quarterly* 4, no. 1 (1988): 194–207.

Harrington, Michael. *The Other America: Poverty in the United States*. New York: Macmillan, 1962.

Harrington, Scott, and Robert E. Litan. "Causes of the Liability Insurance Crisis." *Articles* (February 1988): 737–741.

Harvard Medical Practice Study. *Patients, Doctors, Lawyers: Medical Injury, Malpractice Litigation, and Patient Compensation*. Cambridge, MA: President and Fellows of Harvard College, 1990.

Health Care Financing Administration. *Medicare and Medicaid Data Book, 1988*. HCFA Pub. No. 03270. Baltimore: Department of Health and Human Services, 1989.

Heller, Agnes. *Beyond Justice*. Oxford: Oxford University Press, 1987.

Huber, Peter. "Knowledge of the Law is No Excuse." *Proceedings of the Academy of Political Science* 37, no. 1 (1988): 149–161.

———. "Environmental Hazards and Liability Law." In *Liability: Perspectives and Policy*, edited by Robert E. Litan and Clifford Winston, 128–154. Washington, DC: The Brookings Institution, 1988.

———. *Galileo's Revenge: Junk Science in the Courtroom*. New York: Basic Books, 1991.

Huber, Peter W., and Robert E. Litan. "An Overview." In *The Liability Maze: The Impact of Liability Law on Safety and Innovation*, edited by Peter W. Huber and Robert E. Litan, 1–27. Washington, DC: The Brookings Institution, 1991.

Iglehart, John K. "Health Policy Report: Germany's Health Care System." *New England Journal of Medicine* 324, no. 7 (1991): 503–508 and 324, no. 24 (1991): 1750–1756.

Jackson, Jesse, and Charles Murray. "What Does the Government Owe the Poor? Welfare, Race and the Wealth of a Nation." *Harper's* 272, no. 1631 (1986): 35–46.

Johnson, Joseph E., George B. Flanigan and Daniel T. Winkler. "Cost Implications of No-Fault Automobile Insurance." *Journal of Risk and Insurance* 49, no. 1 (1982): 116–123.

Katz, Jack. *Seductions of Crime*. New York: Basic Books, 1988.

Kozol, Jonathan. *Savage Inequalities: Children in America's Schools*. New York: Crown, 1991.

Kramer, Rita. *Ed School Follies: The Miseducation of America's Teachers*. New York: The Free Press, 1991.

Kriesberg, Louis. *Mothers in Poverty: A Study of Fatherless Families*. Chicago: Aldine, 1970.

Krosney, Richard. *Beyond Welfare: Poverty in the Supercity*. New York: Holt, Rinehart and Winston, 1966.

Lampman, Robert J. *Ends and Means of Reducing Income Poverty*. Chicago: Markham, 1971.

Langlois, Simon, Jean-Paul Baillargeon, Gary Caldwell, Guy Frechet, Madeleine Gauthier and Jean-Piere Simard. *La Société Québecois en Tendances, 1960–1990*. Quebec: Institut quebecois de recherche sur la culture, 1990.

Linton, Adam L. "The Canadian Health Care System." *New England Journal of Medicine* 322, no. 3 (1990): 197–199.

Liska, Allen E., and Barbara D. Warner. "Functions of Crime: A Paradoxical Process." *American Journal of Sociology* 96, no. 6 (1991): 1441–1463.

Litan, Robert E., Peter Swire and Clifford Winston. "The U.S. Liability System: Background and Trends." In *Liability: Perspectives and Policy*, edited by Robert E. Litan and Clifford Winston, 1–15. Washington, DC: The Brookings Institution, 1988.

Mackay, Murray. "Liability, Safety and Innovation in the Automotive Industry." In *The Liability Maze: The Impact of Liability Law on Safety and Innovation*, edited by Peter W. Huber and Robert E. Litan, 191–223. Washington, DC: The Brookings Institution, 1991.

Martin, Robert. "General Aviation Manufacturing: An Industry Under Siege." In *The Liability Maze: The Impact of Liability Law on Safety and Innovation*, edited by Peter W. Huber and Robert E. Litan, 478–499. Washington, DC: The Brookings Institution, 1991.

Mead, Lawrence M. *Beyond Entitlement: The Social Obligations of Citizenship*. New York: The Free Press, 1986.

Mendras, Henri, with Alistair Cole. *Social Change in Modern France: Towards a Cultural Anthropology of the Fifth Republic*. Cambridge: Cambridge University Press, 1991.

Meyer, Marshall W., and Lynne G. Zucker. *Permanently Failing Organizations*. Newbury Park, CA: Sage Publications, 1989.

Moore, Michael J., and W. Kip Viscusi. *Compensation Mechanisms for Job Risks: Wages, Workers' Compensation, and Product Liability*. Princeton, NJ: Princeton University Press, 1990.

Murray, Charles. *Losing Ground: American Social Policy, 1950–1980*. New York: Basic Books, 1984.

———. "White Welfare Families, 'White Trash.' " *National Review* 38, no. 5 (1986): 30–34.

Musto, David J. "Opium, Cocaine and Marijuana in American History." *Scientific American* (July 1991): 40–47.

National Center for Education Statistics. *The Condition of Education 1990*. Vol. 1, *Elementary and Secondary Education*. Vol. 2, *Higher Education*. Washington, DC: U.S. Department of Education, 1991.

National Center for Health Statistics. *Health Insurance and Medical Care: Health of Our Nation's Children, United States, 1988*. Advance Data no. 188. Hyattsville, MD: U.S. Department of Health and Human Services, 1990.

————. *Characteristics of Persons With and Without Health Care Coverage, United States, 1989*. Advance Data No. 201. Hyattsville, MD: U.S. Department of Health and Human Services, 1991.

National Commission on Children. *Beyond Rhetoric: A New American Agenda for Children and Families*. Washington, DC: National Commission on Children, 1991.

National Commission on Excellence in Education. *A Nation at Risk*. Washington, DC: GPO, 1983.

National Conference on Law and Poverty. *Conference Proceedings*. Washington, DC: GPO, 1965.

Olson, Walter. "Overdeterrence and the Problem of Comparative Risk." *Proceedings of the Academy of Political Science* 37, no. 1 (1988): 42–53.

Peet, John. "Health Care: A Spreading Sickness." *The Economist* (July 6, 1991): 3–18.

President's Commission on Law Enforcement and Administration of Justice. *Crime and Its Impact—An Assessment*. Washington, DC: GPO, 1967.

Priest, George L. "Understanding the Liability Crisis." *Proceedings of the Academy of Political Science* 37, no. 1 (1988): 196–211.

————. "Products Liability Law and the Accident Rate." In *Liability: Perspectives and Policy*, edited by Robert E. Litan and Clifford Winston, 184–222. Washington, DC: The Brookings Institution, 1988.

————. "The New Legal Structure of Risk Control." *Daedalus* 119, no. 4 (1990): 207–227.

————. "The Modern Expansion of Tort Liability: Its Sources, Its Effects and Its Reform." *Journal of Economic Perspectives* 5, no. 3 (1991): 31–50.

Rabkin, Jeremy. "Where the Lines Have Held: Tort Claims Against the Federal Government." *Proceedings of the Academy of Political Science* 37, no. 1 (1988): 112–125.

Ravitch, Diane. *The Troubled Crusade: American Education, 1945–1980*. New York: Basic Books, 1983.

Reiser, Stanley Joel. "Malpractice, Patient Safety, and the Ethical and Scientific Foundations of Medicine." In *The Liability Maze: The Impact of Liability Law on Safety and Innovation*, edited by Peter W. Huber and Robert E. Litan, 227–250. Washington, DC: The Brookings Institution, 1991.

Reynolds, Roger, John Rizzo and Martin Gonzalez. "The Cost of Medical Professional Liability." *Journal of the American Medical Association* 257, no. 20 (May 1987): 2776–2781.

Riemer, David Raphael. *The Prisoners of Welfare: Liberating America's Poor from Unemployment and Low Wages*. New York: Praeger, 1988.

Romano, Roberta. "Directors' and Officers' Liability Insurance: What Went Wrong?" *Proceedings of the Academy of Political Science* 37 no. 1 (1988): 67–80.

Rostow, V. P., M. Osterweis and R. J. Bulger. "Medical Malpractice and the Delivery of Obstetrical Care." *New England Journal of Medicine* 321, no. 15 (October 1989): 1057–1060.

Schuck, Peter A. "The New Judicial Ideology of Tort Law." *Proceedings of the Academy of Political Science* 37, no. 1 (1988): 4–17.

Schwartz, Gary T. "Product Liability and Medical Malpractice in Comparative Perspective." In *The Liability Maze: The Impact of Liability Law on Safety and Innovation*, edited by Peter W. Huber and Robert E. Litan, 28–80. Washington, DC: The Brookings Institution, 1991.

Shapiro, Carl. "Symposium on the Economics of Liability." *Journal of Economic Perspectives* 5, no. 3 (1991): 3–10.

Sherraden, Michael. *Assets and the Poor: A New American Welfare Policy*. Armonk, NY: M.E. Sharpe, 1991.

Staaf, Robert J., and Bruce Yandle. "An Incentive to Avoid or Create Risks: Market Share Liability." In *The Economic Consequences of Liability Rules: In Defense of Common Law Liability*, edited by Roger E. Meiners and Bruce Yandle, 81–100. New York: Quorum Books, 1991.

Stevenson, Harold W., and James W. Stigler. *The Learning Gap*. New York: Summit Books, 1992.

Tancredi, Laurence, and Dorothy Nelkin. "Medical Malpractice and Its Effect on Innovation." In *The Liability Maze: The Impact of Liability Law on Safety and Innovation*, edited by Peter W. Huber and Robert E. Litan, 251–273. Washington, DC: The Brookings Institution, 1991.

Todd, Alexandra Dundas. *Intimate Adversaries: Cultural Conflict between Doctors and Women Patients*. Philadelphia: University of Pennsylvania Press, 1989.

Turk, Austin T. *Political Criminality: The Defiance and Defense of Authority*. Beverly Hills, CA: Sage Publications, 1982.

U.S. Bureau of Justice Statistics. *Prisoners 1925–1981*. 1982.

———. *Police Employment and Expenditure Trends*. 1986.

———. *Compendium of U.S. Justice Statistics*. 1986 .

———. *Prisoners in 1986*. 1987.

———. *Report to the Nation on Crime and Justice*. 2d ed. 1988.

———. *Drugs and Jail Inmates 1989*. Special Report. 1989:7.

_____. *Compendium of Federal Justice Statistics, 1986*. 1990.

_____. *Criminal Victimization in the United States 1988*. NCJ-122024. 1990.

_____. *Felony Sentences in State Courts, 1988*. 1990.

_____. *BJS Data Report 1989*. NCJ-121514. 1990.

_____. *Capital Punishment 1989*. 1990.

_____. *NIJ Reports*, no. 221. 1990.

_____. *National Update 1*, no. 1. NCJ-129863. July 1991.

_____. *National Update 1*, no. 2. NCJ-131778. October 1991.

_____. *Violent Crime in the United States*. NCJ 127855. 1991:6.

_____. *Correctional Populations in the United States 1988*. NCJ-124280. 1991

_____. *Race of Prisoners Admitted to State and Federal Institutions 1926–1986*. NCJ-125618. 1991.

_____. *Criminal Victimization in the United States 1989*. NCJ-129391. 1991.

_____. *Criminal Victimization in the United States, 1973–1990 Trends*. 1991.

_____. *Drugs and Crime Facts, 1990*. NCJ-128662. 1991.

_____. *Sourcebook of Criminal Statistics 1990*. NCJ-130580. 1991.

_____. *Prisoners in 1991*. By Tracy L. Morton and Danielle C. Morton. 1992.

_____. *Criminal Victimization in the United States 1990*. NCJ-134126. 1992.

_____. *Prisons and Prisoners in the United States*. NCJ- 137002. 1992.

_____. *National Update 1*, no. 3. NCJ-133097. January 1992.

_____. *Sourcebook of Criminal Statistics 1991*. 1992.

U.S. Bureau of the Census. *Historical Statistics of the United States: Colonial Times to 1970*. Part I, series B28–35. Washington, DC: GPO, 1975.

_____. *Characteristics of Households and Persons Receiving Selected Noncash Benefits 1983*. Series P–60, no. 148. Washington, DC: GPO, 1985.

U.S. Congress. House. Committee on Energy and Commerce. *Automobile Insurance*. Serial no. 100–151. 1988.

_____. *Automobile Insurance*. Serial no. 101–113. 1989.

_____. *Federal Employers' Liability Act*. Serial no. 101–109. 1989.

U.S. Congress. House. Committee on the Judiciary. *Oversight Hearing on Corrections, Overcrowding and Alternatives to Incarceration*. Serial no. 59. Washington, DC: GPO, 1989.

U.S. Congress. Joint Economic Committee. *The Cost of the Tort System*. 99th Cong., 2d sess., S. Hrg. 99–1090.

U.S. Congress. Senate. Committee on Finance. *Data and Materials Related to Welfare Programs for Families with Children*. Washington, DC: GPO, 1988.

U.S. Congress. Senate. Special Committee on Aging. *Unnecessary Surgery: Double Jeopardy for Older Americans*. 99th Cong., 1st sess. GPO Serial no. 99–1, 1985.

U.S. General Accounting Office. *Medical Malpractice: A Framework for Action*. GAO/HRD-87–73. 1987.

————. *Relationships and Incomes in Households with AFDC Recipients and Others*. GAO/HRD-88–87. 1988.

————. *Health Insurance: Bibliography of Studies on Health Benefits for the Uninsured*. GAO/HRD-89–27FS. February 1989.

————. *Health Insurance: An Overview of the Working Uninsured*. GAO/HRD-89–45. 1989.

————. *Health Care: Initiatives in Hospital Risk Management*. GAO/HRD-89–79. 1989.

————. *Health Insurance: Cost Increases Lead to Coverage Limitations and Cost Shifting*. GAO/HRD-90–68. May 1990.

————. *Canadian Health Insurance: Lessons for the United States*. GAO/HRD-91–90. 1991.

————. *Health Services: Available Research Shows that Capacity Is Only Weakly Related to Volume*. GAO/PEMD-91–7. 1991.

————. *Off-Label Drugs: Reimbursement Policies Constrain Physicians in Their Choice of Cancer Therapies*. GAO/PEMD-91–14. 1991.

Useeum, Bert, and Peter Kimball. *States of Siege: U.S. Prison Riots, 1971–1986*. New York: Oxford University Press, 1989.

Virginia Health Planning Board. *Access to Obstetrical Care*. Senate Document No. 27. Richmond, VA, 1990.

Viscusi, W. Kip. "Liability for Occupational Accidents and Illnesses." In *Liability: Perspectives and Policy*, edited by Robert E. Litan and Clifford Winston, 155–183. Washington, DC: The Brookings Institution, 1988.

————. "Product and Occupational Liability." *Journal of Economic Perspectives* 5, no. 3 (1991): 71–91.

Watts, James. "A Survey of Indiana School Corporations: General Liability Insurance and Practice: 1982–1986." Ph.D. Diss., Indiana University, 1989.

Wedemeyer, J. M., and Percy Moore. "The American Welfare System." *California Law Review* 54, no. 2 (1966): 326–356.

Weiler, Paul C. *Medical Malpractice on Trial*. Cambridge, MA: Harvard University Press, 1991.

Williams, C. Arthur, Jr. *An International Comparison of Workers' Compensation*. Boston: Kluwer Academic Publishers, 1991.

Williams, Terry. *The Cocaine Kids: The Inside Story of a Teenage Drug Ring*. Reading, MA: Addison-Wesley, 1989.

Wilson, James Q., ed. *Crime and Public Policy*. San Francisco: ICS Press, 1983.

Wilson, James Q., and Michael Tonry. *Drugs and Crime*. Vol. 13. Chicago: University of Chicago Press, 1990.

Wilson, William Julius. *The Truly Disadvantaged: The Inner City, the Underclass, and Public Policy.* Chicago: University of Chicago Press, 1987.

Yandle, Bruce. "Rules of Liability and the Demise of Superfund." In *The Economic Consequences of Liability Rules: In Defense of Common Law Liability*, edited by Roger E. Meiners and Bruce Yandle, 143–158. New York: Quorum Books, 1991.

INDEX

About the Author

THEODORE CAPLOW is Commonwealth Professor of Sociology at the University of Virginia. He is the author of many journal articles and books on this subject.

ISBN 0-275-94911-7

90000>

EAN

9 780275 949112

HARDCOVER BAR CODE